Time for Assessment

Evaluation Tips with Six New Learning Centers

by Dana McMillan

illustrated by Janet Armbrust

Teaching & Learning Company

1204 Buchanan St., P.O. Box 10
Carthage, IL 62321

This book belongs to

_____

Cover by Janet Armbrust

ISBN No. 1-57310-046-3

Printing No. 98765432

Teaching & Learning Company
1204 Buchanan St., P.O. Box 10
Carthage, IL 62321

Table of Contents

Dear Teacher,

Several years ago I was asked to present a **two-hour** workshop for a staff of early childhood teachers about assessment practices. It was an impossible task to cover such an encompassing (and often controversial) topic as assessment in that time frame. To add to the concern, I was told shortly before the workshop was to begin that the teachers were in the process of trying to persuade their school board to drop standardized tests for the youngest children in the district. At the time, many of the board members had no idea what the research said about the abuses of standardized tests. This issue had been greeted with a cold shoulder from most of the board and even from some district administrators.

The memory of this workshop stands out to me mostly as one of frustration. In many ways I was "preaching to the choir" in my concerns about standardized tests. But an even greater frustration was that the teachers could not hear any ideas about developing their own assessment program when they were still in a battle to see the formal testing program abolished.

Several weeks after the workshop, I received a small children's book entitled *First Grade Takes a Test* by Miriam Cohen from one of the participants. The teacher who sent the book, wrote an inscription that suggested this book might help me put into words for other groups of teachers what I had been trying to say in the workshop. Since then, I have never done a workshop/consulting with early childhood educators on assessment without first reading this book. The question the book always suggests to me is this: *Do young children know when they are being formally assessed?* Every early childhood teacher I have ever asked this question has answered a resounding YES!

This book is dedicated to the idea of an assessment program being designed by the people who know the child best and with the child's perspective in mind. I hope it is helpful for you as you work out your own developmental assessment program.

Sincerely,

Dana

Dana McMillan

Chapter 1
Overview of Assessment and the Young Child

A Developmentally Appropriate Assessment Program

A Developmentally Appropriate Program is one that understands the child's stage of development and his/her individual and unique development and plans a program around those issues.

A Developmentally Appropriate *Assessment* Program should:
- compare the child only to himself
- be ongoing
- have a design that is informal

Those three simple elements will guide the thinking of this book and all of the activities that are included as examples. Let's examine them more carefully.

Compare the Child Only to Himself:

Standardized assessment programs are designed to compare groups of children. The information gained demonstrates only how a group of children in one district compare to another group at that time. It is, at best, a snapshot. If we accept that children develop through predictable stages (based on the work of Jean Piaget), but at their own pace, then any assessment that we do should not see how the child differs from others, but should look for the areas where the child is making progress in her own learning.

Ongoing:

The major concern developmental educators have expressed about formal assessment programs is that they are given once a year and only provide information about the cognitive skills in some areas. An ongoing program uses the information that children show us for every area of their learning and is continual. It looks at what a child knows early in the school year and compares that to subsequent work. It also reminds us that the nonacademic times can provide valued information.

Informal:

Expecting young children to sit quietly and fill in bubbles on a paper-and-pencil test is in direct contrast to an informal assessment program. We should assume that the teacher knows what she wants to see about what a child knows and she will find a way to document that learning without making the child feel like he is "performing for an adult."

TLC10046 Copyright © Teaching & Learning Company, Carthage, IL 62321

What Is the History of Assessment Programs?

In her book, *Achievement Testing in the Early Grades: The Games Grown-Ups Play*, Constance Kamii provided an insight into how standardized testing took control of our early childhood programs.

Before 1950 few people who completed high school took more than three standardized tests their entire school careers. The results of such tests were hardly ever discussed. Parents didn't receive the scores, and school-wide results certainly never appeared in the newspaper.

Prior to 1965 tests were not often used in the early grades. There was consensus associated with the traditions that gave rise to the kindergarten, as well as to the subsequent developmental beliefs guiding the primary grades as whole, that the early years were "special," a time for natural growth and development. Where serious testing programs existed, they generally began in third or fourth grades.

In 1989 students who completed high school took 18 to 21 standardized tests during their school careers. Considerable attention was paid to the preparation for the test. Many students heard admonitions about "doing your best" and "how important this test is to you and to our school."

Definition of Terms Associated with Assessment

Standardized Assessment	Empirically selected items Norm or criterion reference Data on reliability and validity Commercially produced
Nonstandardized Assessment	Systematic observations Anecdotal records Checklist and collections Developed by the teacher
Developmental Screening Test	Assesses a child's level of preparedness for a specific academic program
Diagnostic Assessment	Identifies child with specific needs Determines the nature of the problem
Intelligence Test	Measures cognitive functioning Often used in diagnostic assessment

According to the National Association for the Education of Young Children (NAEYC) position statement of standardized testing of young children (1987), no single test can be used for all purposes, rarely will a test be applicable to more than one or two areas.

Some Examples of the Baby Book Theory in the Classroom

Vital Statistics:

The teacher develops a sheet with information about the things the families do together, likes and dislikes of the child, important people in the child's life, etc. This form should be easy and fun for a family to fill out together.

Developmental Milestones:

Ask the parents when the child took his first step, said his first words, etc. Then share with the parents that you will both be watching for new milestones in his language, writing, social and physical development.

Samples of Work:

When the child has a product she is especially proud of, ask her, "Would you like to put this in your own special file so that we can look at it later and remember how special this was?" Put a date on the work to help you remember when it was added to the file. If the child seems hesitant to part with the work and wants to take it home, make a copy for the file. With time, children will become more comfortable with the idea of putting work in their files.

Some Examples of the Baby Book Theory in the Classroom

Treasures, Mementos:

Make a tape recording or videotape of children as they share a special item that they have brought to school. Take a picture of a child holding a special memento, with a favorite block structure or with a completed work of art.

Anecdotal Notes:

Develop the habit of carrying a small notebook with you as you interact with children during learning center or cooperative learning time. Jot down notes about what you see the children doing. Describe interests they show, how they work out problems, what things get them off track. Place the notes in the child's file for review and reminders as you prepare for evaluations and parent conferences.

Record of Gifts:

In the traditional baby book, parents keep a record of gifts children receive. It may be important for a teacher to know what gifts children receive (or do not receive). Are the gifts appropriate for the child? Special family traditions or religious practices are information that teachers need to be aware of, too.

Understanding How Children Construct Knowledge

If learning were as simple as being given a step-by-step sequence for how to master a skill, then we could ignore the information about construction knowledge. But it is not. Consider how this familiar skill was acquired.

How did you learn to drive a car?

You rode in a car.

You had a toy car to play with.

You may have had an opportunity to sit in the driver's seat and experience the feel of the steering wheel.

You had friends who began to drive cars and it looked like an appealing thing to do.

You enrolled in driving instruction class.

You were given a textbook with an enormous amount of information about cars, rules for driving, restrictions, diagrams and charts.

Your parents let you back the car out of the driveway.

You went for your first experience of driving a car on the road with the instructor guiding you from the front passenger seat.

You practiced driving many times.

You took your written and behind-the-wheel driving test and passed both.

You became a competent driver.

Look over this list and consider:

- What if you did the first two and then skipped to driving on the road?
- What did playing with the cars do for you later in the learning?
- What if you had never been in a car when you went to the driving instructor?
- What if the instruction had only been written information?

Now consider how your learning could be assessed at every stage, rather than only with the final assessment of taking a driving test.

A Theoretical Framework for Developing an Appropriate Assessment Program for Young Children

The following guidelines must be considered in planning an appropriate assessment program according to the National Association for the Education of Young Children and the National Association of Early Childhood Specialists in State Departments of Education.

Children learn best when their physical needs are met and they feel psychologically safe and secure	Children should not be expected to sit for long periods of time and perform paper and pencil tasks
Children construct knowledge	From infancy, children are mentally and physically active, struggling to make sense of the world
Children learn through social interaction with adults and other children	One example: Language development is fundamental to learning and language development requires social interaction
Children's learning reflects a recurring cycle that begins in awareness and moves to exploration, inquiry and finally, utilization	Any new learning by children follows this relatively predictable cycle
Children learn through play	Spontaneous play provides opportunities for exploration, experimentation and manipulation that are essential for constructing knowledge
Children's interests and "need to know" motivate learning	Activities that are based on children's interests provide intrinsic motivation for learning

The following is a list of words to describe a commonly found item. Read the list carefully and see if you can name the thing they describe.

Vital Statistics
Developmental Milestones
Important Events
Educational Information
Family History
Medical Records
Samples of Artwork
Treasures
Mementos
Favorite Things
Anecdotal Notes and Records
Record of Gifts
Current Events
Religious Information

What is this common item? Look on the next page . . .

The Baby Book Theory of Assessment

The list on the previous page was developed by a group of teachers when they were asked to describe a baby book. Look over the list and ask yourself this question: *Is there anything on this list that a teacher would not need to know about a child in her classroom?*

What if you could develop your own assessment program using a baby book as your theoretical base?

What do you think about when you consider a baby book?
- Personal to the child
- Shows the child's development but not any comparisons to others
- Provides memories
- Is enjoyable to look over, time and time again

Picture a family, mother, father and five-year-old child, entering a kindergarten room at the beginning of the school year. They appear to be a little nervous as they enter the room to meet the teacher. Unexpectedly, the parents produce the child's baby book. They hold it out to the teacher and say: "Here is our daughter's baby book. We've kept it since before she was born. Now, as she begins school, we know that we will both be placing information in her book–you, as her teacher and we, as her parents. We want to share it with you."

That is the theory behind a Developmentally Appropriate Assessment Program.

Putting It Together:
How Children Construct Knowledge

Using the list from page 9 as an example, make your own list with an outcome often found among educational objectives. Choose one outcome and describe all of the steps necessary for mastery of the outcome. Next to each step of the learning, think about a way that you could see that the child is making progress toward the outcome.

List of possible outcomes:

The child is competent in understanding numbers.
The child understands coins and their values.
The child uses writing to communicate.
The child understands measurement.

List of Steps to Develop the Outcome	Assessment

Chapter Summary
Discussion Questions

This page is designed to help you clarify your thinking after having read Chapter 1.

What are your feelings about standardized tests for young children?

_____

_____

_____

_____

_____

What are the implications for a teacher-designed assessment program?

_____

_____

_____

_____

_____

What statement would you write to express your personal beliefs about how young children learn?

_____

_____

_____

_____

_____

How does a statement of beliefs about learning contribute to a school's assessment plan?

_____

_____

_____

_____

_____

Chapter 2
Designing an Assessment Program for Young Children

Creating Your Own Assessment Program

Before you begin to create your own developmentally appropriate assessment program, you must consider these key questions:

- What do you as the teacher want to know about what your children know?

  _____

  _____

  _____

- What do the parents of the children in your classroom want to know about what their children know?

  _____

  _____

  _____

- How can you learn about more than just the cognitive skills that are developing in each of your children?

  _____

  _____

  _____

- What educational decisions will you need to make as a result of the assessment program you design?

  _____

  _____

  _____

Four Areas of a Child's Development

An assessment program should include all four areas of each child's development.

Language:

Including speaking, listening, questioning, labeling, writing and reading

Cognitive:

Problem solving, observing, predicting outcomes, understanding concepts

Physical:

Large and small motor

Social/Emotional:

Creating, role playing, negotiating, flexibility, understanding feelings

Four Categories of Learning

Learning can be organized into four categories as described by Lillian Katz in her article "What Should Young Children Be Learning," from the ERIC Clearinghouse on Elementary and Early Childhood Education, Urbana, Illinois.

Knowledge:

In early childhood, knowledge consists of facts, concepts, ideas, vocabulary and stories. A child acquires knowledge from someone's answers to his questions, explanations, descriptions and accounts of events as well as through observation.

Skills:

Skills are small units of action which occur in a relatively short period of time and are easily observed or inferred. Physical, social, verbal, counting and drawing are among a few of the almost endless number of skills learned in the early years. Skills can be learned through trial and error, observations, instructions, directions and coaching; and they improve with drill and repetition.

Feelings:

These are subjective emotional states, many of which are innate. Among those that are learned are feelings of competence, belonging and security. Feelings about school, teachers, learning and other children are acquired in the early years.

Dispositions:

Dispositions can be thought of as habits of the mind. Curiosity, friendliness or unfriendliness, bossiness and creativity are dispositions rather than skills or pieces of knowledge. There is a significant difference between having writing skills and having the disposition to be a writer. Dispositions are not learned through instruction or drill. The dispositions that children need to acquire or strengthen are learned from being around people who exhibit them. It is unfortunate that some dispositions, such as being curious or puzzled, are rarely displayed by adults in front of children.

Putting Four Areas of Development Together with Four Categories of Learning

The following were taken from a Kindergarten Progress Report Card. Look at what types of learning we assess and in what areas. Also look at what we don't assess.

Objective	Knowledge	Skill	Feeling	Disposition
Knows birthday	X			
Recognizes name	X			
Writes to 5		X		
Counts to 5		X		
Identifies colors	X			
Follows verbal directions		X		
Can jump		X		
Catches a ball		X		
Uses pencil grip		X		
Colors in lines		X		
Uses scissors correctly		X		
Traces a pattern		X		
Names numbers	X			
Walks on balance beam		X		
Can march		X		
Can hop		X		
Prints first name		X		
Says alphabet	X			
Counts to 20		X		
Writes to 10		X		
Uses left to right		X		
Sorts correctly	X			
Classifies correctly	X			
Positions words	X			
Uses simple graph	X			
Knows shapes	X			
Draws shapes		X		
Knows days of the week	X			
Identifies lengths	X			
Repeats simple rhyme		X		
Skips		X		
Sequences		X		
Knows phone number	X			
Knows address	X			
Knows coins	X			
Recognizes rhymes	X			
Recognizes sight words		X		
Recognizes beginning sounds		X		
Recognizes ending sounds		X		
Matches upper and lowercase		X		
Knows seasons of the year	X			

Assessing Children's Feelings and Dispositions

As the previous page shows, we do a competent job of assessing knowledge and skills. How do we document the development of the child's feelings and dispositions? First we must find the types of activities where these can be seen. Then observations and anecdotal records may be the most effective method for assessing them.

When in an educational setting, will children demonstrate feelings and dispositions?

Choice Times:

Learning centers, recess, cooperative learning activities (if children are allowed to make real choices), choosing a book

Informal Times:

Lunch, snack, transition between activities, playground, cleanup time

Social Times:

During informal conversations between children, while playing a game, waiting for an activity to begin or at the end of the day

Interactions with Adults:

Conferences with children, working together on a project, negotiating with children during a conflict

Methods of Observing Children

There are several methods that can be used for making systematic observations of children. The key is to choose a method that will work for you and to stay with that system. If observing children is new to you, go slowly, adding a new method only after you are secure with the first.

Anecdotal Notes:

Use note cards or a small notebook that you can keep with you during an activity period. Notes will be valuable for many purposes, including when you see a child who has figured out a new skill, mastered something that you know they have been working on or shown an interest in something new. Be sure to put the date, the child's name and a few key sentences that will serve as a reminder for later. Place the notes in the child's file.

Observation Forms:

A premade form is a valuable method for making notes about a common activity. Forms can be developed for writing observations about group games, choosing books, setting the tables for snacks or following directions in a cooperative learning project.

Stages of Development Forms:

Using stages of development for making observations serves as a reminder about where children are in the predictable sequence of development. For example: There are clear stages of play, block buildings or writing development.

Checklists:

Checklists may be developed and kept for individual children in a specific area where definite skills are demonstrated and mastered. Math skills and language development may lend themselves to checklists.

The following pages have samples of each of these methods for observing children.

Sample of Anecdotal Records

Language Example:

Jerrod showed Peter how to finish his spaceship using all verbal directions, very concerned about going in a logical order.

Nov. 21

Cognitive Example:

During a game of tens, Katie demonstrated several times that she can now add two numbers by counting on from the larger playing card. Will watch for more signs of numerical understanding.

Dec. 2

Physical Example:

Marcus is still using both hands for writing, drawing and other small motor activities. Watch closely for dominance to develop.

Oct. 24

Social/Emotional Example:

Juan and Michael had a major conflict over what to build with the blocks. I tried not to step in. They didn't solve it the way I might have, but they did manage to reach a compromise.

Mar. 15

Sample of an Observation Form

Observing Children Playing a Group Game

The Game: _____

The Players: _____

_____

_____

_____

1. How did the players decide which game tokens they would use?

   _____

   _____

2. How did the players decide who would go first, second, etc.?

   _____

   _____

3. How consistent were they in determining the number of spaces to move?

   _____

   _____

4. Did the players take turns as agreed?

   _____

   _____

5. What signs of cooperation were demonstrated?

   _____

   _____

6. Which child emerged as the leader of the group? What methods did he/she demonstrate?

   _____

   _____

Stages of Writing Development

Child's Name: _____

Stage 1: Scribbling

Date: _____

Stage 2: Linear Drawing

Date: _____

Stage 3: Letter-Like Forms

Date: _____

Stage 4: Letter and Early Word Symbols

Date: _____

Stage 5: Invented Spelling

Date: _____

Stage 6: Standard Spelling

Date: _____

Sample of a Checklist

Literacy Development Checklist

Child's Name: _____   **Date of Birth:** _____

Development Area	**Begin**	**Secure**

Book Awareness
Listens to stories
Shares reading with others
Selects books to look at
Holds book correctly
Turns pages in sequence
Examines pictures
Asks for books to be read

Comprehension
Recalls main idea
Recalls details of story
Names events from story
Understands cause/effect

Reading Behavior
Attempts to read along
Reads from pictures
Turns pages at appropriate time
Knows where the print is on the page

Print and Word Awareness
Begins to match words
Tracks to find a word
Recognizes common words in print
Awareness of letter and sound
Recognizes letter names in words
Talks about his own reading behaviors
Transfers reading behavior from known
    to unknown materials

Text Reading
Reads familiar, predictable text
Reads unfamiliar text
Reads a variety of types of books
Chooses to read

Favorite Books

List the child's favorite books below.

Book   **Date read**

_____   _____

_____   _____

_____   _____

_____   _____

_____   _____

_____   _____

_____   _____

_____   _____

_____   _____

_____   _____

_____   _____

_____   _____

Setting Up Tasks for Making Observations

Choosing appropriate tasks that will allow you to make observations of children in all four areas of development is one of the most demanding jobs in creating an assessment program. The following are some examples:

Language Development:

Children's choices of books, reading together, writing original stories, discussing artwork, describing the sequence for completing an activity, putting labels on a block structure.

Example: Two boys are working together at a table. Each has been given the assignment of writing a script for a movie about whales. While they work, you overhear their conversation. Notice the interactions and what it tells you.

Tom, a strong reader, asks James if he will help him illustrate his story when it is complete. Tom explains, "You're the best artist in the room." Some time later, James asks Tom how to spell *desperate*. You are somewhat surprised that James knows the word, but clearly he is able to use it correctly in a sentence: *The whale is desperate to get back out to the ocean*. You consider the exchange earlier with Tom. Did Tom's complement to James' artistic ability give James some measure of self-esteem in asking for help with a new word?

The key in this task is that the children are allowed to work on their own, but not in isolation, they work at the table where they can interact with each other. During this task, we can make several observations about the language abilities of both boys and also about some social skills that are developing.

Setting Up Tasks for Making Observations

Cognitive Development:

Group games where children decide on strategies, use math skills, work a puzzle, work at a sand and water table, cook, use a survey to make a graph, use a math manipulative to solve problems, work with real animals, plants.

Example: Su Lin and Corey are playing a game of tic-tac-toe. The first conflict arises as they decide who will go first. Corey suggests that he should because he might not get to again. Su Lin considered that as a possibility but then says they should choose in a way that is fair to them both. She suggests they use "bumble-bee, bumblebee." Corey accepts that idea but when he loses, he quickly says that he should get to go first anyway. They have reached an impasse, when Su Lin suggests that she will go first this game and Corey can go first the next. Corey accepts this idea and play begins.

When two young children play a game like the one described above, the teacher has the opportunity to observe how children solve real problems. Su Lin demonstrated her skills in suggesting compromise to facilitate the play. Corey may not be as far along in this skill, but the opportunity to work with Su Lin may help promote this for him. The teacher could have stepped in and made the decision for them, but an opportunity for observing problem-solving skills would have been lost.

Physical Development:

Large motor activities such as kicking a ball, playing a game of catch, walking a balance beam, jumping rope, skipping and climbing. Small motor skills include cutting out pictures from a magazine, writing on lined paper, putting puzzle pieces in the proper spot, sewing, stringing beads and using a stapler.

Example: Trevor is very interested in sewing a purse for his mom. He has chosen a small needle and very fat yarn and encounters the dilemma of not having success in threading the needle. He asks you to thread the needle for him. You suggest that he can thread it himself but that he should choose either a smaller piece of yarn or a larger needle. He willingly finds a new type of thread and finds that he is able to thread the needle.

When a child is very motivated to do something, he may challenge himself to develop a skill that otherwise might not appear. Left alone, however, this child might have become so frustrated that he would have given up his idea of making the present for his mother. The teacher's suggestion saved him some frustration, but she resisted the request to thread the needle for him. Helping him to discover that with the right combination of needle and thread he could do it himself was a better solution. It kept the project the child's (and not the adult's) and left the teacher able to observe the subsequent developments.

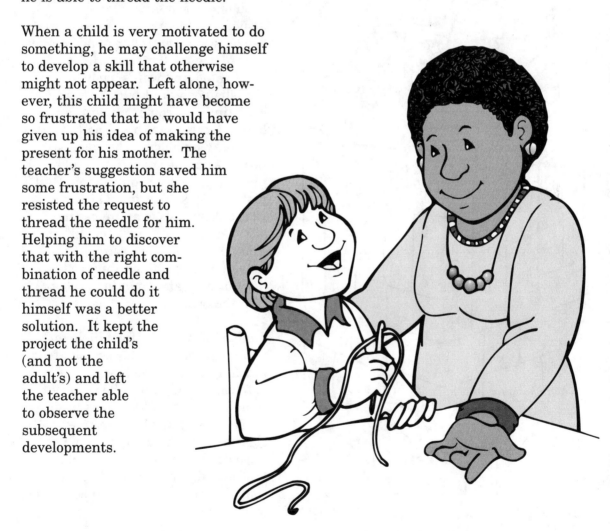

Setting Up Tasks for Making Observations

Social/Emotional Development:

Creating roles in dramatic play; playing with puppets or dolls; building things that are known to them with blocks, Legos™, or other building materials; using a box for dramatic play; creating a solution with other children and playing out the roles.

Example: Tanisha is determined to build a "tall building" with the unit blocks. She encounters a series of difficulties. The first develops when she has almost figured out how to make a second story. Patrick arrives in the Block Center and with one swish, knocks down her structure. She is mad for a minute as she stands with her hands on her hips glaring at Patrick. He seems undaunted and walks away. Tanisha goes right back to the task. This time she comes up with a much better strategy for building the second story by placing the same size blocks as corner pieces and then placing a flat piece on the top. But just then Josh shows up at the Block Center. She assumes the worse and yells, "Don't touch!" at him. Josh asks very softly, "Can I help?" Tanisha allows him to help her but only after making it clear, "I'm the boss."

Tanisha is a determined little girl. Although the obstacles seemed too much at times, she showed this determination both in her desire to complete the task she had set for herself and in dealing with her classmates. The episode may not have demonstrated every social grace we might hope for but clearly that is developing and will serve her well in the future.

Chapter Summary
Discussion Questions

This page is designed to help you clarify your thinking after having read Chapter 2.

What do you want to know about what the children you work with are learning?

_____

_____

_____

_____

_____

How many of the things on the list are knowledge or skills? How do you know about children's feelings and dispositions?

_____

_____

_____

_____

How do you make time in the school day for observing children and making anecdotal notes about each child for whom you are responsible for?

_____

_____

_____

_____

Write a brief observation that gives you information about the child's learning.

_____

_____

_____

_____

Defining Terms Associated with a Theme-Based Program

The following terms and their definitions will assist you in understanding the design of this chapter and the chapters to follow.

Integrated Curriculum:

A curriculum designed around a theme or topic instead of isolating the subject areas.

Themes:

A topic (theme) is chosen which is an area of interest to the children and which allows the teacher to design a variety of projects that exercise skills in every area of a child's development.

Projects:

Projects are tasks or activities that support the theme. Ideally, they consist of more in-depth work which allows one or more children to work toward a process—not just a product.

Starting Points:

An introduction to the theme that develops children's interest in the area they will be studying and gives the teacher an opportunity to assess what information the children may already have.

Resources:

A rich variety of materials gathered in an area that is easily accessible to the children to support the theme. Resource materials include books and other printed matter, puzzles, puppets, dramatic play materials and other real-life objects.

What Does Thematic Teaching Have to Do with Assessment?

A truly integrated curriculum and the full development of a theme is an ideal setting for an appropriate assessment program for young children.

If the theme is chosen around the interests of the children that you work with—instead of dictated by workbooks, textbooks or even the teacher—you have an opportunity to see what knowledge children bring to the theme.

If children have a chance to study and work in areas that are interesting to them, they are intrinsically motivated. This allows the teacher to see the child in that type of learning environment as opposed to one that requires the child to follow the interest and lead of the teachers.

What Does Thematic Teaching Have to Do with Assessment?

More in-depth work on projects allows the teacher to learn more about a child's feelings and dispositions (see page 16 of Chapter 2) as well as her interactions with other children and her ability to stay with a task for more sustained periods of time.

Since the outcomes of many projects are varied, the work that children will produce will span a wide range as well, allowing the teacher to see a more detailed picture of the children's development in a variety of areas.

When more time is spent on a theme, the teachers may find that the children's knowledge about the theme deepens. Teachers who become comfortable in this way of working are often surprised to find that the children want to know much more about the theme than they might have originally anticipated.

Choosing a Theme

Before you begin planning a theme, gather the children around a chart stand with blank chart paper and ask this question:

"If we could choose to study anything, what would you like to learn about?"

Encourage the children to discuss a variety of topics and record their responses on the chart paper with their name beside their contribution. As contributions are offered, read back the entire list. Ask questions for clarification. For example, if a child says they would like to learn about animals, you might ask, "There are lots of kinds of animals, is there one kind that you especially would like for us to learn about?" For older children, you may leave the chart paper available for several days and encourage the children to continue to add topics they may think of as they work.

What We Would
Like to Learn About

bugs—Patrick
ponds—Moesha
birds—Miguel
Grandmas—Analise
big road trucks—Joe

Choosing a Theme for Young Children

Once you have used the process described on the previous page to discover what types of things children are interested in learning about, you may want to consider categorizing and narrowing or broadening them to begin to create a meaningful theme. Consider the following theme categories:

Themes Related to Children:

Homes, babies, families, food, school, toys, games, grandparents, TV, clothes

Themes Related to the Community You Live In:

Community helpers, shops, transportation, airport, hospital, fire fighters, post office, big machines, building sites, manufacturing plants, farming, mining

Themes Around Local Events:

Carnival, circus, Olympics, sports, holidays, local celebrations, art festivals, famous people, rodeo

Themes About Places the Children Know:

Neighborhood, roads, bridges, fountains, shopping areas, landmarks, rivers, lakes, woods, mountains, oceans

Themes About Natural Events the Children Relate To:

Weather, plants, gardening, nature centers, animals, zoo, snow, rocks, insects, dinosaurs, beaches

General Information Interesting to the Children:

Ships, inventions, toys, space travel, simple machines, exotic animals, puppets, books, hats

Creating a Theme Web

The next step in developing a theme is to plan for the types of learning and activities that will guide the theme. The process described below is one of several that will help you do this effectively. Ideally, it is done with several of your teaching colleagues who are interested in sharing the process of developing a theme.

1. Begin with a brainstorming time by giving each person a stack of index cards. Work quietly alone to write as many ideas as possible about the theme, one idea per card. Work for about 10 minutes.

2. Share the cards with the group. Combine any that say the same thing or have the same idea. Lay all of the cards out on a flat surface where every member of the group can see them.

3. Decide on categories and organize the cards under each category heading. Agree as a group to discuss differences in ideas and compromise when necessary. Place the cards in two categories if necessary. Continue to add cards to categories as you think of them.

4. Transfer the cards onto a large sheet of paper in the form of a planning web. Add stories, resources, field trips and project ideas. This becomes a permanent record for reference throughout the theme.

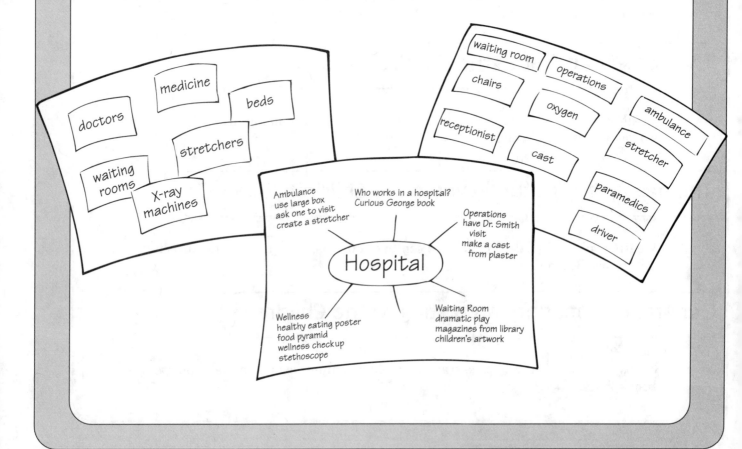

Designing Meaningful Starting Points
for Themes

Think broadly about a starting point. Traditionally we have used a book to introduce a theme. But what could you design that would give you feedback about what information the children bring to the theme?

When the children enter the room on Monday morning, they discover the teacher draped over a beanbag chair moaning loudly. She is dressed in a large wrinkled shirt with candy bar wrappers sticking out of the pockets and empty cans of soda laying about her. She has curious red marks on her face and arms and dark circles under her eyes.

- The teacher can begin a discussion with the children about their opinions on why she doesn't feel well.

- The children can contribute to a chart about what makes a person healthy or unhealthy. This chart can be placed in a visible place for reference during the theme.

- The children can take turns playing the role of the health professional and give the teacher a checkup. The teacher can ask questions such as, "Doctor, what should I do to get rid of these red dots?"

- The children can work in pairs to make a *before* and *after* poster of the teacher showing what she needs to do to make herself healthy.

More Examples of Starting Points

Another Example for a Theme on the Body:

Arrange for the school nurse to visit the children and allow them to listen to each other's heartbeat with a stethoscope. Afterwards make a chart about what they know about their heart and what it does for their body. On a separate sheet of chart paper, make a list of what they would like to know about other parts of their body. Hang the charts in the classrooms where they can be referenced throughout the theme.

A Starting Point for a Theme on the Post Office:

Ask a class of older children to write a letter to each child in your classroom. Place the letters in individual envelopes with the child's name on each. Pack all of the letters into a large box and take it to the post office for regular mail delivery. Arrange for the box to be delivered to the classroom. Make the box's contents a mystery. Encourage the children to try to figure out who sent the box by looking at clues: return address, the stamp, the cancellation mark. Once inside, allow the children to assist in determining the best method for delivering each child's letter and how to figure out what the letter says and who sent it to them. Afterwards, make a chart about what the children know about the mail and how it gets delivered and what things they would like to know more about. Hang the charts in the room where they can be referenced throughout the theme.

A Starting Point for a Theme on the Water:

Give each child a Styrofoam™ cup with an ice cube inside. Ask the children some general questions about ice cubes, what they are made out of and what makes them melt. Give each child a marker and ask them to put their name on the cup and choose a place in the room where they think their ice cube will melt quickly. Record on chart paper each child's name, where they placed their cup and ice cube and how long they predict it will take for their ice cube to melt completely. Read a beginning book about water. For example: *The Underwater Alphabet Book* by Jerry Pallotta. At the end of the book, ask the children to check their cups and compare the results to the chart and their predictions. Help the children draw some conclusions about their ice cube and what contributed to the melting.

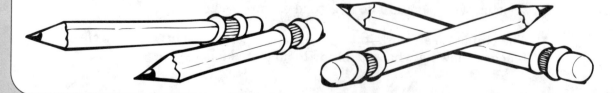

Designing Projects Around a Theme

A project (or task) should develop the children's interest in the theme and provide the teacher with additional information about what the children know. The following are issues to consider in designing projects.

Consider the Time Frame:

We often think that a project should be completed by the children in a short period of time, evaluated and taken home to the family refrigerator by the end of the same day. Consider developing projects that allow the children to spend a longer part of a day or even days. Some projects may allow them to work on a draft and come back to the project for revisions. In assessing this type of work, you will be able to see children's dispositions toward their work, the ability to stay with a task, to look for solutions and work to completion.

Consider Using Small Groups:

Designing projects that allow children to work together in small groups gives you a new area of assessment we have not had traditionally. This way of working allows us to see children interact with each other, express their opinions and negotiate with the others in the group. The cooperative learning research has demonstrated the need for children to have dispositions that allow them to work together rather than in competition. Designing projects that develop this way of working is one way of achieving it.

Consider Open-Ended Projects:

As you are designing projects for a theme, try to make as many of them as possible open-ended, where the process is the critical attribute rather than the product. In assessing children's work in this type of project, you will discover more about their interests and creativity.

Hints About Making a Theme Successful

Timing:

You may not know for sure how long a theme will take to complete. Some teachers think of a theme as being a week of work. If you leave the timing more open-ended, you may discover that the longer you allow children to work on a topic the more in-depth the learning becomes.

Groups:

One successful way of working with children during a theme is to place them in heterogeneous groupings that work together throughout the theme. In this way the children have time to learn to work together. Allow each group to give themselves a name that relates to the theme. Make a chart with the names of the groups and the children who are in that group. Post the chart in the area of the classroom where you do whole group instruction about the theme (a starting point, for example) and where projects will be discussed.

Whole Group Time vs. Small Group Time:

Young children can tolerate only small doses of whole group instruction. Try to balance those times with more time in small groups, learning centers and project times. Don't assume that the children cannot do any "work" on the theme until you have "taught" it to them. Children will learn much about the theme and develop many other skills in well-chosen projects done in small groups.

Scheduling the Projects:

Consider having each small group do a different project each day. The benefit to this way of working is that you can balance the types of projects. Combine one or two that will demand more teacher time with those that require less. If you discuss the projects with the entire class both before they begin work and after the work is completed, all of the children will hear about the project. This will help children build their ideas from work done by other groups. The schedule in this visual shows the projects from Chapter 4, The Body theme.

Project	Group 1	Group 2	Group 3	Group 4
Healthy Plate of Food (page 44)	Monday of Week 1	Friday of Week 1	Thursday of Week 1	Wednesday of Week 1
Parts of the Body (page 46)	Tuesday of Week 1	Monday of Week 1	Friday of Week 1	Thursday of Week 1
Building a Hospital (page 47)	Wednesday of Week 1	Tuesday of Week 1	Monday of Week 1	Friday of Week 1
Healthy Practices Poster (page 48)	Thursday of Week 1	Wednesday of Week 1	Tuesday of Week 1	Monday of Week 1
Baby Hospital (page 54)	Friday of Week 1	Thursday of Week 1	Wednesday of Week 1	Tuesday of Week 1

Don't forget to be flexible when you are scheduling projects for children. A schedule like the one above is a must for working out your plans, but those plans will often change. One project may take longer to complete than you anticipated. One day may be disrupted by a special event at the school. To accommodate the unexpected, consider having one day scheduled for "catching up" on projects.

Chapter Summary
Discussion Questions

This page is designed to help you clarify your thinking after having read Chapter 3.

What are the benefits of an integrated curriculum?

_____

_____

_____

_____

If you asked the children in your classroom about their interests and what they would like to learn, how would they respond? Do we assume that we know what topics they would be interested in studying?

_____

_____

_____

_____

Choose a theme to web as a test case. Follow the procedure on page 36. What worked for you and what would you change the next time?

_____

_____

_____

_____

As you consider potential themes for your classroom, consider resources that are available to you. Make a draft of potential themes for a year cycle, and note any special resources you currently have available.

_____

_____

_____

_____

Chapter 4
The Body

A Healthy Plate of Food

Materials:

variety of colors of playdough
rolling pins
variety of tools for working with play dough, plastic
    knives and forks, cookie cutters
paper or Styrofoam™ plates
index cards
crayons or markers

Preparations:

Prepare a sur-
face appropriate
for working
with play dough
by covering a
table with
butcher or art
paper. Gather
the materials
described above.

Before You Begin:

Discuss a healthy meal with the children. Read a book
about good eating habits. Make a chart of the types of food
that we should have at each meal.

Implementation:

Ask the children to use the play dough to mold different foods they would like to display on a plate to show a healthy meal. Encourage the children to choose a well-bal-
anced meal. When their plate is completed, allow them to use the index cards to
label their foods, assisting them as necessary. Display the plates for future discussions.

Assessment:

Knowledge of foods and healthy meals, small motor skills to use the tools. Language
and communication in interactions with other children while they work and labeling
connections. Feelings about healthy eating practices.

A Skeleton

Materials:

model of a skeleton (Check with a local natural history museum, high school or library to see if you can have one on loan for the theme.)

poster of a human skeleton (if you cannot secure an actual model)

straws

scissors

black construction paper

white glue

Preparations:

Gather the materials at a working space with the model of the skeleton or poster in easy access to the space.

Before You Begin:

Show the children the skeleton and identify some of the major bones, for example, the long bones of the arms and legs and the rib cage. As you show them the various bones, ask them to feel the same bones on their body. Explain that the straws will be bones in a picture they will make of a skeleton by gluing the straws in place on the paper.

Implementation:

Allow the children to work at their own pace to complete a skeleton with the straws. Provide a place for the glue to dry completely. Help each child print his or her name on their picture and display the skeleton. Use the pictures for future discussions about the skeleton.

Assessment:

Knowledge about the skeletal system of the body, small motor skills in cutting and gluing the straws in place, language and interactions in labeling the bones and interacting with other children while they work.

Parts of the Body

Materials:

large roll of art paper
variety of markers
resource books on a child's level
about the body

Preparations:

Gather the materials in the area of the classroom where the children can work in a small group on the floor with markers.

Before You Begin:

This activity is a good assessment activity which can be done several times during the topic of the body. In the beginning of the theme it will provide you with information about what knowledge children bring to this theme. Later on it will help you see what children are learning about their bodies.

Implementation:

Ask the children to work together as a group to draw around one child. Use the markers to put in all of the parts of the body they know about in the correct location. Allow the group to share their work with the class and encourage them to point out the various parts of the body they identified in their work. Display each group's work in an area where you can use it for future discussions throughout the

Assessment:

Knowledge about the parts of the body and location. Language and communication in working with others on a project. Dispositions to stay with a group task, negotiation skills and sharing ideas with others.

Building a Hospital

Materials:

set of building materials
   (Legos™, for example)
index cards and markers
resource books with information about hospitals
chart paper and markers

Preparations:

Gather the materials in an area of the classroom where the children can work with the
building materials successfully.

Before You Begin:

Ask the children to help make a list on chart paper of the parts of a hospital. Once
complete, explain that they will work in groups to build one part of the hospital, one
group at a time. When they are finished, they will have a completed hospital. If
they do not have permanent groups for the theme, divide the children into working
groups and ask the first group to choose from the list on the chart paper the part of
the hospital they would like to work on. Print the names of the children in that
group (or their group name if they have one) next to the part of the hospital they
choose to build.

Implementation:

Allow the children in each group to work together to build their part of the hospital. Once completed, assist them in making a label for it with an index card folded
in half. When all of the parts of the hospital are complete, add small people and
transportation toys for dramatic play.

Assessment:

Knowledge about the parts and functions of a hospital. Language and communication skills to interact with group members, negotiation skills in expressing their
opinion. Small motor skills in using building materials. Disposition to stay with a
group task and work out problems.

Healthy Practices Poster

Materials:

white typing paper
pencils
construction paper
markers
resource books about
    healthy practices

Preparations:

Introduce and read one or more books that will give the children some background about healthy practices.

Implementation:

Give each child a sheet of white paper and ask them to make a draft of a poster that shows two or more healthy practices. Encourage the children to work at an area where they can exchange ideas. When the draft posters are finished, have conferences with children to clarify their ideas, assist with writing and make suggestions. Next, give each child a sheet of construction paper and markers to complete the poster in final form. Once completed, allow each child to discuss the poster with the other children and display posters for others to enjoy.

Assessment:

Knowledge about healthy practices. Language and communication skills to express ideas in pictures and words. Disposition to stay with task from draft through completion and the ability to implement suggestions into their work.

Building an Arm

Materials:

collections of odds and ends, for example: packing materials, small boxes, Styrofoam™, sponges, fabrics, yarn, string, variety of paper
white glue
model of a skeleton or poster (see materials on page 45)

Preparations:

Collect the materials in an Art Center where children can use them and other items that are available in the center.

Before You Begin:

Lead a short discussion about how the arm works. Ask the children to look carefully at their arm and encourage them to examine how the arm moves and bends. Explain that they will be working at the Art Center to build an arm that works the same way their arm works. Let them choose to work with another child or alone.

Implementation:

Allow the children to work through the process of creating an arm out of odds and ends. Encourage them to think about ways they can make a wrist and arm with open-ended questions about how the arm does various tasks. For example: "Could your arm throw a ball?" This project may take a long period of time. You should allow children to work on their project and put it aside to come back to later, as necessary. On completion, encourage children to share their arm with the class and display them for future reference throughout the theme.

Assessment:

Knowledge of the functions of the arm. Skills to use a variety of art materials. Disposition to persist with an open-ended task, to work with others, use materials in new and interesting ways and to solve problems.

Healthy Practices Survey

Materials:

chart paper and markers
class list with pictures
clipboards and pencils
colored pencils
art paper

Preparations:

Make a display showing the children in your classroom and label with each child's name and picture. Display it where it can easily be seen by the children.

Before You Begin:

Ask the children to help brainstorm a list of healthy practices. Record the list on chart paper with markers.

Implementation:

Working with one small group of children at a time, ask the group to decide on one of the healthy practices on the list to turn into a survey question. For example: If the children listed brushing teeth on the chart, they could make a survey question that says, How many times each day do you brush your teeth? Assist the children in determining how they could organize the survey and use the class list to see that they have asked the question of every child in the room. Accept their input, making suggestions where necessary. Provide the clipboards and allow the group to work through the process of asking the questions and recording the responses. After the survey is complete, lead a group discussion with the children about compiling the information for presentation to the class. Provide art paper and markers and encourage the children to make their presentation in a form that will be understandable to others, allowing them to make decisions about how they will accomplish the task. Allow the group to make a presentation showing the results of the survey. Choose another group to repeat the process on another healthy practice from the list.

Assessment:

Knowledge of healthy practices, designing a survey, recording information, making information understandable for others, use of a wide range of language and math skills, working with others on a project, contributing to a group, dispositions of working with others, problem solving and staying with a task.

Measuring Your Foot

Materials:

art paper
scissors
crayons or colored pencils
graph paper with 1" (2.5 cm) squares
Unifix™ cubes
white glue

Preparations:

Gather the materials at a table where a small group of children can work comfortably.

Before You Begin:

This project is best designed for one small group of children to work through at a time and may take more than one day for completion.

Implementation:

Lead the group in a brief discussion about the measurements of various parts of their body. For example: their arms, legs, circumference of their heads and the length of their feet. Ask the children to remove their shoes and use art paper to draw around one foot with a crayon. Ask each child to cut out the foot shapes. Have them compare the length with one another. For more comparisons, allow the children to use Unifix™ cubes to show the length of paper. Provide each child with a section of graph paper. Ask them to show the number of Unifix™ cubes they had for the length of their foot by coloring the corresponding squares on the graph paper. Cut out the length of squares and compare them to others. Ask the group to make a chart to show the other children the results of their group's measurements from the shortest to the longest foot. Provide a large sheet of art paper, colored pencils, crayons and glue, and allow the group to work out a plan for displaying their graph. Provide assistance with writing as necessary. Encourage the group to present their graph to the class and mount the chart for future reference through-out the theme.

Assessment:

Knowledge about measurement; sequencing; counting; skills in small motor of coloring squares, cutting and using glue. Language and communication skills in working with a group, negotiating with others, making their ideas known and developing methods for displaying their results effectively.

Measuring Your Foot

Step 1: Each child traces a foot on art paper and cuts it out with scissors.

Step 2: Use Unifix™ cubes to show the length of the foot.

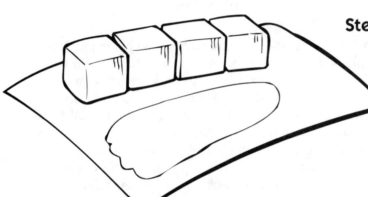

Step 3: Place the Unifix™ cubes on 1" (2.5 cm) graph paper and color in the corresponding number of squares.

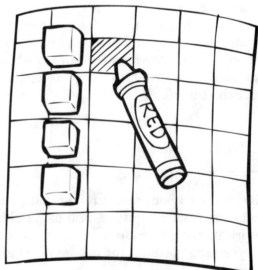

Step by Step for Measuring Your Feet

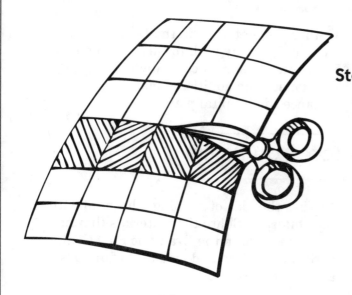

Step 4: Cut out the strip of colored-in squares of graph paper and compare it to the length of the feet of the other children in the group.

Step 5: Work together as a group to make a chart showing the results of their work.

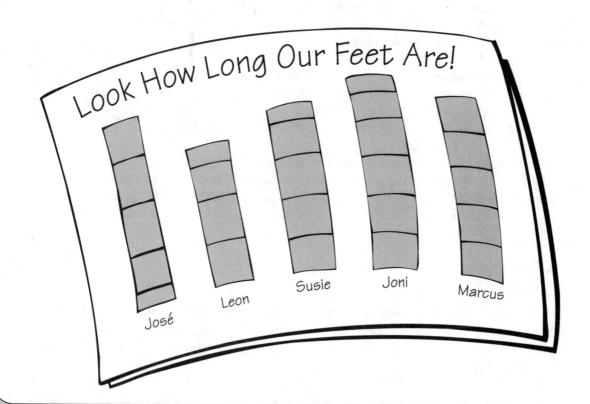

Look How Long Our Feet Are!

José   Leon   Susie   Joni   Marcus

Baby Hospital

Materials:

dramatic play equipment: baby beds and blankets, baby bottles, baby food jars, dolls, stuffed animals, shelves, table, chairs,
hospital equipment: stethoscope, bandages, doctor's lab coats, empty medicine bottles, tongue depressors
writing materials for making signs
clipboards, paper and pencils
scale
measuring stick

Preparations:

Gather the materials in the Dramatic Play Center. You may wish to check with a medical center or supply company to see if they can donate any additional materials to enhance the hospital play.

Before You Begin:

Discuss the idea of running a hospital with the children. Share the materials that have been gathered in the Dramatic Play Center with the children and lead a brief discussion about their uses.

Implementation:

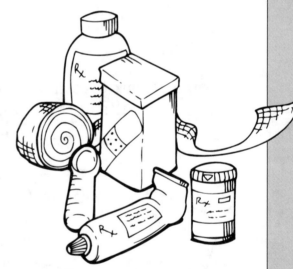

Allow one small group of children to work in the Baby Hospital at a time, providing health care to dolls and stuffed animals. Encourage the children to design the space with patient care and reception areas set up as they see workable. Encourage the children to take on roles as doctors, nurses and receptionists. For older children, a treatment sheet may be duplicated and attached to clipboards. Add information on the form about weight and height for children to have a practical application for using a scale and measuring stick. At the end of each working period, allow the children who worked in the Baby Hospital to describe the day's work. Share the treatment sheets and discuss illnesses and treatments. As play continues over the course of the theme, encourage the children to make a sign for the hospital and label materials on shelves.

Assessment:

Knowledge about hospitals, illnesses, treatments and measurements of height and weight. Language skills of interacting with other children, completing written forms, negotiating and expressing their opinions. Dispositions of working cooperatively and taking on roles.

TLC10046 Copyright © Teaching & Learning Company, Carthage, IL 62321

Baby Hospital Treatment Sheet

Name: _____

Height: _____ Weight: _____

What is wrong?

_____

_____

_____

_____

_____

_____

_____

Treatment:

_____

_____

_____

_____

_____

_____

_____

_____

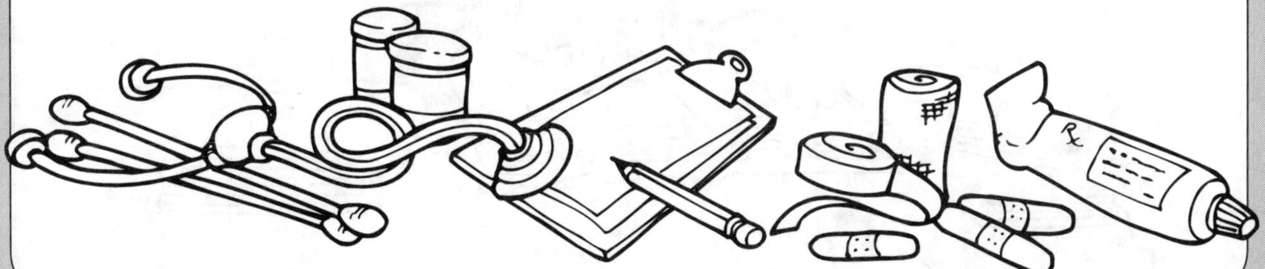

Resource Books for the Theme
The Body

Alligator Arrived with Apples: A Potluck Alphabet Feast, Aladdin Books, 1992

Bread and Jam for Frances, Russell Hoban, Harper & Row, 1964

Ears Are for Hearing, Paul Showers, Thomas Crowell, 1990

Eric Needs Stitches, Barbara Pavis, Lippincott, 1979

Germs Make Me Sick, Melvin Berger, Thomas Y. Crowell, 1985

Going to the Hospital, Fred Rogers, Putnman's Sons, 1986

A Hospital Story, Sara Bonnett Stein, Walker, 1974

I Can Be a Doctor, Rebecca Hankin, Children's Press, 1985

Madeline, Ludwig Bemelmans, Puffin Books, 1939

The Magic School Bus, Inside the Human Body, Joanna Cole, Scholastic, 1989

My Doctor, Harlow Rockwell, Macmillan, 1973

My Feet, Aliki, Harper & Row, 1990

My Hands, Aliki, Harper & Row, 1990

Nutrition, Leslie Jean LeMaster, Children's Press, 1985

Rita Goes to the Hospital, Martine Davison, Random House, 1992

What's Inside? My Body, Dorling Kindersley, 1995

When I Eat, Mandy Shur, Carolrhoda Books, 1992

Why Do I Eat? Rachel Wright, First Aladdin Books, 1992

Your Heart and Blood, Leslie Jean LeMaster, Children's Press, 1984

Your Insides, Joanna Cole, Putnam & Grosset, 1992

Your Skeleton & Skin, Ray Broekel, Children's Press, 1984

Wrapping Boxes

Materials:

variety of boxes
brown wrapping paper or newsprint
tissue paper
masking or strapping tape
string
scissors
markers
stickers or trade stamps

Preparations:

Gather the materials in an area where one group of children can work together.

Before You Begin:

Divide the children into groups and allow them to give their group a name associated with the theme. (See page 40 in Chapter 3 about working in groups.) Choose a book about the post office from the list of resource books on page 69. Wrap the book in tissue paper, place the book in a box that disguises it as a book and wrap the box in wrapping paper. Address the box to the class and place a stamp on the box. If possible, ask someone from the office to deliver it during your class meeting.

Implementation:

When the box is delivered, lead a short discussion about the possible contents. Lead the children into a discussion about the address, stamp and how the box was wrapped. Open the box and read the book to the group. Then allow one group at a time to work in the area where the materials are gathered. Ask them to choose an item from the room to send to another group. Ask them to wrap the box and address it. If necessary, post a sign in the area with the names of the groups and their members. At the end of each work period, allow the group to deliver their package to the addressee. Use this opportunity to point out how the box was wrapped, addressed and delivered. Continue until each group has had at least one opportunity to wrap a box. Or plan to leave the wrapping area available to the children throughout the theme.

Assessment:

Knowledge of written language, measurement and knowledge of sizes for boxes and paper for wrapping. Small motor skills in using materials. Ability to tie and knot. Language and communication skills in working with others in the group, written language and expressing their ideas. Dispositions to work cooperatively, negotiate and to communicate with others.

Sorting Junk Mail

Materials:

variety of junk mail, magazines and used envelopes
shoe boxes

Preparations:

Before beginning the Post Office theme, write a letter to parents explaining the theme and some of the learning you expect to occur as a result. Ask the parents to send in junk mail, old magazines, cancelled stamps (to be used in subsequent projects) and used envelopes. You may also check with your school's office, local businesses or the post office in your area for materials that will be helpful in this project and others.

Before You Begin:

Lead a short discussion about how the mail must be sorted in the post office before it can be delivered. Ask the children some open-ended questions about how they think that postal workers would determine how the mail is delivered. Encourage discussion between the children and accept the answers as possible solutions.

Implementation:

Put a variety of junk mail in an area where a small group of children can work sorting the mail. Provide shoe boxes for sorting trays. Allow the children to work together to decide the categories for the mail and to negotiate a difference in opinion. At the end of the time, encourage the group to discuss their categories and how they determined them with the rest of the group.

Assessment:

Knowledge about categories, sorting. Language and communication skills in sorting, labeling and discussing them with other children in the group. Dispositions to persist with an open-ended task and negotiate with others.

The Mailbox

Materials:

enough small boxes for each child to have their own mailbox (for example: shoe, check or cereal boxes will work)
paper
stickers
white glue
scissors
peel-off labels
markers

Preparations:

Gather the materials in the Art Center where additional art materials are available.

Before You Begin:

Discuss the idea of the children each having his or her own mailbox in which to receive mail. Lead a discussion about the possible results of their having a place for mail. Include in the discussion how the mailboxes should be labeled and where they should be located in the classroom.

Implementation:

Allow one small group at a time to work on decorating their mailboxes using materials in the Art Center. Assist the children in printing their name on the peel-off label, as necessary. Once the mailboxes are completed, you may want to secure them with strapping tape or mount them on a wall at a level appropriate for the children. The mailboxes will be important for other projects throughout this theme.

Assessment:

Knowledge about names, addresses and labels. Skills in using art materials. Dispositions toward artwork, working cooperatively with other children and persisting to complete a task.

Stamp Collections

Materials:

variety of cancelled stamps
photo albums with peel-back pages

Before You Begin:

If possible, invite a person whose hobby is stamp collecting to come to the class and show some of his or her books and display of stamps. Encourage the children to look for information about stamp collecting and ask questions of the guest speaker. You might check with the local post office for resources on stamp collections.

Assessment:

Knowledge of categories and labels. Small motor skills in working with the stamps and album pages. Dispositions to work cooperatively and to take pride in their work.

Preparations:

See *Sorting Junk Mail* on page 59 for ideas about collecting a variety of cancelled stamps. Gather the stamps and albums at a table where a small group of children can work together.

Implementation:

Allow one small group to work together to create a stamp album. Encourage the children to decide how to display the stamps on the pages in the album. At the end of the work time, allow the group to share their stamp album with the others in the class. Encourage questions about how they organized their stamps and promote that as a discussion with the entire class. For example, you might ask: "How did you decide to put these stamps on a page together?" Each group may start over from the previous group by taking the stamps out of the album and making their own display.

Designing Stationery

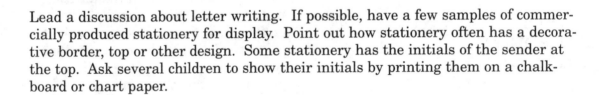

Materials:

white typing paper
markers
crayons
variety of stamps and ink pads
white envelopes

Preparations:

Gather the materials
listed above at a table
or in the Writing
Center.

Before You Begin:

Lead a discussion about letter writing. If possible, have a few samples of commercially produced stationery for display. Point out how stationery often has a decorative border, top or other design. Some stationery has the initials of the sender at the top. Ask several children to show their initials by printing them on a chalkboard or chart paper.

Implementation:

Allow one small group to work on the project at one time. Ask the children to use the materials to make their own stationery. Encourage the children to decorate several sheets of paper with a design of their own choosing. Once completed, the stationery may be used in other projects for writing letters.

Assessment:

Knowledge about initials of their name. Small motor skills in using the art materials. Language and communication skills in discussing projects with other children. Disposition to take pride in artistic work.

Class Address Book

Some families are sensitive about sharing address information in classroom settings. Therefore, this activity may not be appropriate for some classrooms.

Materials:

lined paper
cover stock (poster board,
    file folders, etc.)
pencils
chart paper
markers

Preparations:

Add a number to the label of each child's mailbox. (See *The Mailbox* project on page 60.) Make pre-made blank books by stapling several sheets of lined paper to one sheet of cover stock. See the diagram. Print each child's name on the cover.

Before You Begin:

Lead a short discussion about addresses. Encourage the children to share what they know about why we have a home address. Allow children to share their address if they know it. Show an address book and talk about when you use one. Tell the children that you have put a number on each of their class mailboxes. Allow them to go to the mailboxes and find their number.

Implementation:

Allow the children to make their own address book, using the blank book you made described in the Preparations phase. Working in small groups, allow the children to decide the best method for gathering and recording the addresses of the other children in the room. Encourage the children to decorate the front cover of their books as they wish. Share the completed books with the class. At this point children may think to use the stationery they made (described on page 62) to write letters to classmates to be mailed in the class mailboxes.

Assessment:

Knowledge of addresses, their own and others and beginning alphabet skills may be noted. Small motor skills in writing names and addresses. Feelings of pride in a completed project.

Class Post Office

Materials:

variety of real materials to turn the Dramatic Play Center into a post office
Dressing the part: man's blue shirt, blue knee socks, large leather purse (mailbag), official hat or one that is similar
Designing the space: stamps, envelopes, scale, city maps, junk mail, sorting bins, zip code directory, postcards, pens and markers, boxes, brown wrapping paper, cash register, phone

Preparations:

Gather the materials described above with any additions to make the Dramatic Play Center feel like a post office.

Before You Begin:

If possible, visit your local post office and have one of the staff give the class a tour, pointing out the various areas that are found in the post office. After you return, lead a short discussion about the visit. Make a list of things the children saw. Bring out the materials that you have collected and discuss them.

Implementation:

Allow one small group of children to work in the Post Office at a time, providing ample opportunity for them to work out how to set it up and create roles for themselves. Encourage the children to write letters and take them to the post office to buy stamps, weigh and send packages, and to have mail delivered to their mailbox. This area will continue to develop throughout the theme.

Assessment:

Knowledge about the roles of the post office and workers. Skills in sorting, labeling, reading and writing, communicating with others effectively. Dispositions to take on a role, work with others cooperatively, design a work environment, discuss and negotiate.

Post Office Forms

Make copies of these forms for the Class Post Office (described on page 64).

Change of Address Form

Name: _____

Address: _____

_____

_____

New Address: _____

_____

_____

Hold Mail Form

Name: _____

Address: _____

_____

_____

Hold my mail on this day: _____

Postcards

Materials:

index cards
magazines (travel magazines will be helpful
   for pictures of places to visit)
scissors
white glue
examples of postcards

Preparations:

Gather the materials at a table where a small
group of children can work comfortably. Make
a display of old postcards to give the children
some ideas of the kinds of things they could
put on their postcards. Make a copy of the
back side of the postcard from page 67 to display along with the old postcards.

Before You Begin:

Use the postcard display to lead a short discussion about making postcards. Include
in the discussion reasons for sending postcards and how postcards are addressed.

Implementation:

Ask a small group of children to work on
designing their own postcards using pictures from magazines or their own
designs. Encourage the children to
address the postcards and send them
through the Class Post Office (see page
64). If they wish, the postcards can be
taken home to mail to a friend or relative.
Find opportunities to talk with the children about their efforts. Ask open-ended
questions about their choice of pictures.
Assist, if necessary, in helping them write
a message and address on the back.

Assessment:

Knowledge of concept of writing a message, sending mail,
places to visit. Language and
communication skills in
expressing thoughts in written
form (use the Stages of
Writing Development form on
page 22), use of conventional
writing for addresses.
Feelings about accomplishing
a project. Disposition to complete a written work.

Postcards

Make copies of the postcards below. Fill in an address and display with old postcards.

Dear _____,

_____

_____

_____   To: _____

_____

_____   _____

From: _____   _____

Dear _____,

_____

_____

_____   To: _____

_____

_____   _____

From: _____   _____

Constructing a Post Office

Materials:

unit blocks
paper and pencils
scissors
toy wooden and plastic cars
toy wooden and plastic people

Preparations:

Gather materials in the Block Center.

Before You Begin:

This project will be more effective after having taken the class on a visit to the local post office. Lead a short-discussion about how the children could build a post office in the Block Center.

Implementation:

Allow one small group of children to work in the Block Center at a time. Encourage them to work together to design a post office by using the blocks. Ask open-ended questions about their design and to encourage them to add new areas to their building. For example: "Could you make a place for people to mail their letters from their cars?" Add the small plastic cars and people to the project for dramatic play. Encourage the children to make signs for their building and cut paper into small pieces for pretend mail.

Assessment:

Knowledge about the parts of a post office. Small and large motor skills in using the blocks and other materials. Language and communication skills in expressing their ideas to others. Dispositions to work cooperatively, take on roles and problem solve.

Resources for the Theme
The Post Office

Dear Mr. Blueberry, Simon James, Margaret K. Elderry Books, 1991

Don't Forget to Write, Martina Selway, Ideals Children's Books, 1994

Hail to Mail, Samuel Marshak, Holt, 1990

Hi, Ann Herbert Scott, Philomel Books, 1994

Here Comes the Mail, Gloria Skurzynski, Bradbury Press, 1992

The Jolly Christmas Postman, Janet Ahlberg, Little Brown & Co., 1991

I Want to Be a Postal Clerk, Eugene Baker, Children's Press, 1976

Marvels of U.S. Mail, Oren Arnold, Abelard-Schuman, 1964

Mail Critters, Mercer Mayer, Simon & Schuster, 1987

No Mail for Mitchell, Catherine Siracusa, Random House, 1990

Mr. Griggs' Work, Cynthia Rylant, Orchard Books, 1989

The Post Office Book, Gail Gibbons, HarperTrophy, 1982

The Postman, Rosalinda Kightley, Macmillan, 1987

The Postal Workers A to Z, Jean Johnson, Walker & Co., 1987

The Prince Who Wrote a Letter, Ann Love, Child's Play, 1992

Special Delivery, Betty Brandt, Carolrhoda Books, 1988

Toddlecreek Post Office, Uri Shulevitz, Farrar, 1990

A Trip to the Post Office, Fisher-Price, 1987 (video)

A Visit to the Post Office, Sandra Ziegler, Children's Press, 1989

Chapter 6
Water

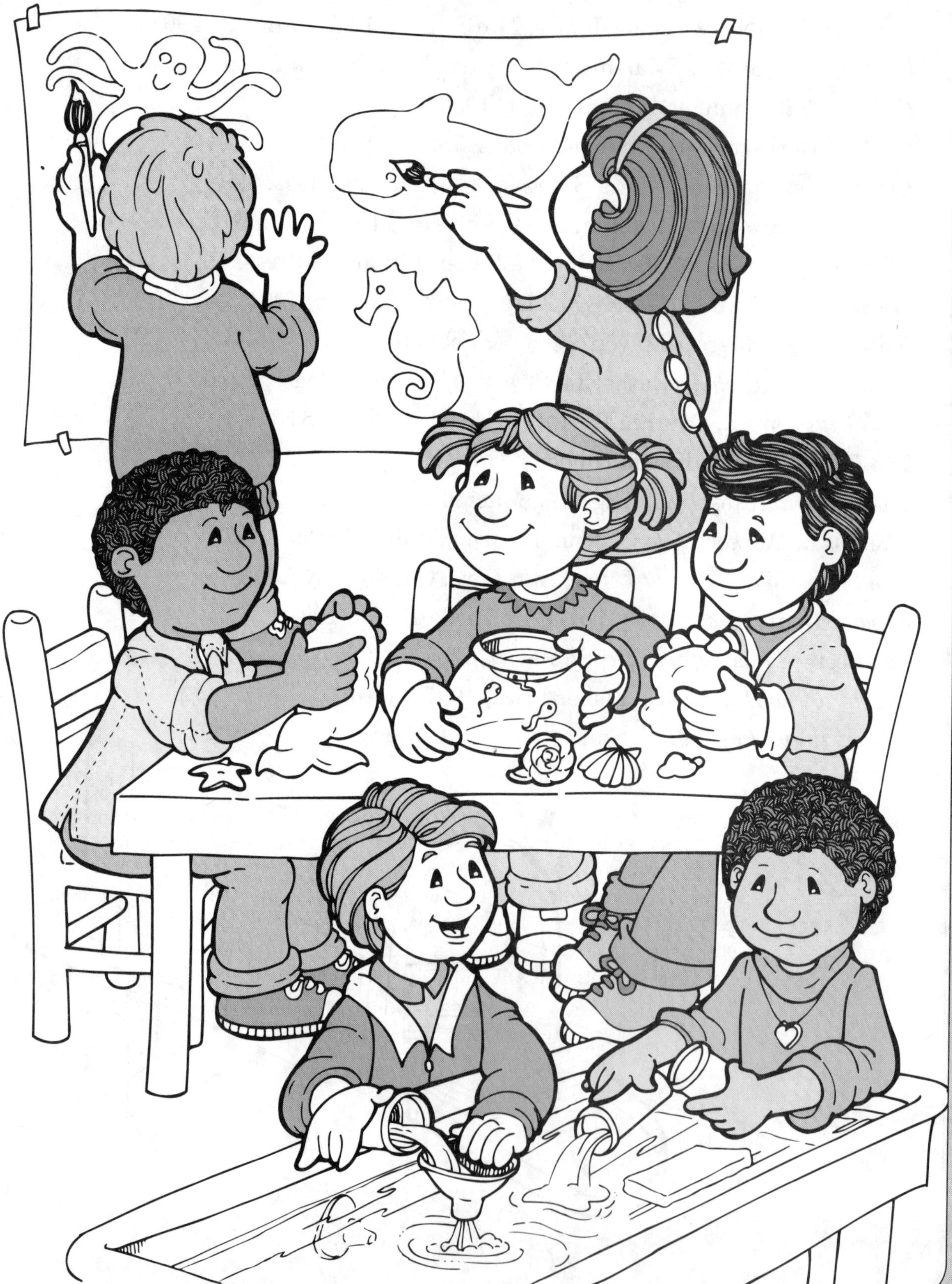

What Does Water Do?

Materials:

chart paper and markers
copy of page 72
pencils, colored pencils, crayons

Preparations:

Provide your school librarian or local library with a copy of the resource list on page 83. Ask them to locate as many of the books listed as possible. Select a book to read to the children that gives an overview of water and the different resources it provides.

Before You Begin:

Read the book to the children. Lead a short discussion about water and why we need it. Make a list of their suggestions on chart paper under a caption: *What does water do for us?*

Implementation:

Work with one small group at a time. Review the list from the chart with the children and ask them to make any additions they think of. Gather the children at a table where they can work cooperatively. Provide each child with a copy of page 72, pencils, colored pencils and crayons. Ask the children to choose four different things that water does for us from the list and draw a picture on their sheet. Allow each child to make his or her own decisions about what to depict in each box. As they work, ask the children if they need any written captions that you can provide. Encourage the children to interact with each other about their pictures and why they choose them. Once completed, allow each child to show the paper to the class and display the pages for reference throughout the theme.

Assessment:

Knowledge about the functions of water. Language and communication skills in expressing ideas on paper, and interactions with other children about their work. Dispositions to stay with a task to completion and pride in the finished product.

What Does Water Do for Us?

Water Investigations

Materials:

sand and water table or several sturdy
   plastic dishpans
plastic dish drainer
paint smocks or large size shirt
funnels in a variety of sizes and shapes
measuring cups

Preparations:

Prepare a place in the classroom
where this activity can take place
throughout the theme. Cover a table
with a plastic tablecloth or painter's
drop cloth and cover a section of the
floor. Place the sand and water table
on top. Place the materials gathered
in a plastic dish drainer.

Before You Begin:

Lead a short discussion about the different things children can discover when they
work with water. Introduce the various materials in the area. Discuss the rules for
working with water. For example: The number of children who may work at one
time, wearing a smock or paint shirt over clothes, cleanup procedures.

Implementation:

Time for free exploration will be critical for this project. Allow each group ample
time to use the materials in the water. The critical role of the teacher is to ask open-
ended questions about the water explorations as the children are working. For
example: "Can you fill a container more quickly with this funnel than that one?"
You may also find it valuable to spend a few minutes with each group in observing
their play but not interupting with questions. At the end of each session, encourage
them to discuss their findings with the class.

Assessment:

Knowledge about mea-
surement, water flow
and comparisons. Skills
in pouring and reading
measurements.
Dispositions to work
with others, play in a
cooperative manner, to
stay with an open-ended
explorations and discuss
their findings with the
teacher and classmates.

Water Investigations Follow-Up Activities

Use these activities in subsequent weeks as a follow-up to the initial exploration project described in Water Investigations on page 73.

Investigation with Sponges:

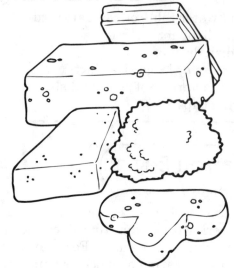

Add a variety of sizes and types of sponges to the water exploration area. Encourage the children to measure the amount of water a sponge can hold and compare to other sponges. Older children may chart their results and display the results in the area where the water explorations are being done.

Investigation of Floating:

Add several flat Styrofoam™ or plastic dishes and small plastic animals to the water exploration area. Encourage the children to investigate how many plastic animals can float on the top of one of the dishes before it sinks.

Investigation with Tubes:

Add plastic tubing to the water exploration area. Allow the children to make discoveries about how water moves through a tube. Add a bucket to the area to see if the water can be transported from the water table to the bucket. Encourage the children to discuss their discoveries.

Assessment:

Knowledge about measurement, comparisons, actions of water and graphing. Skills in reading numbers on a measuring cup and counting. Language in discussing work and discoveries, displaying findings in a graph. Dispositions to explore with new materials, make discoveries, persist with a task and interact with other children.

Water Animals

Materials:

chart paper and markers
variety of colors of clay or dough
tools for working with clay or dough: plastic knives,
    forks, rolling pins and a cutting board to work on
paper plates
blue tissue paper
white glue
index cards

Preparations:

This project may work best in the Art
Center where the materials listed
above have been gathered and other
materials available in the Art Center
are provided.

Before You Begin:

Lead a brief discussion about animals that live in water. Make a chart of the
children's suggestions. Post the chart in the Art Center for reference for this and
other projects throughout the theme.

Implementation:

Ask the children to make an animal that lives in the water from clay or dough.
Encourage them to use the list of animals from the chart for ideas about what
animals they might like to mold. Give each child a paper plate and blue tissue paper
to make a mini water display for their animal. Fold an index card in half and allow
the child to print the name of their animal on it or assist them if necessary. Display
the animals throughout the theme for further discussions and references.

Assessment:

Knowledge about animals that live in the water. Labels for animals and their habitats. Small motor skills in using tools. Language and communication skills in discussing their work and printing the animal names. Feelings of pride in an art project. Disposition to persist with a task.

Water Animal Murals

Materials:

large roll of art paper
magazines (children's science magazines are a
 good source for pictures of animals)
scissors
white glue
paints

Preparations:

Gather the materials listed above in an area suited for children to work with art materials and where a wall space is available for work on a mural. Place a sheet of the art paper on the wall at a level convenient for one group of children to work at a time. You will make one mural for each group.

Before You Begin:

Lead a short discussion about animals that live in the water. If you have done the Water Animals on page 75 you may use the chart that the children generated in that project to assist in the discussion. Read a resource book about animals that live in the water.

Implementation:

Allow one group at a time to work together to make murals. Ask the children to use the magazines to find pictures of animals that live in the water. Ask them to cut out the pictures and glue them onto the art paper. Provide paints for the children to add more details to the mural. Encourage them to think about what animals they might find in the habitat they have created and add them to their mural. For example, you could ask, "What could the fish in your mural have to eat? Could you paint that on your mural?" When the mural is complete, print the names of the children in the group along the top or bottom and provide time for the group to share their mural with the class and discuss their work. As each group completes a mural, leave it on display for future reference throughout the theme.

Assessment:

Knowledge about animals and their habitats. Language and communication skills in expressing their work and communicating their ideas, working out ideas with other group members in a cooperative project. Small motor skills in cutting, using glue and paints. Feelings about a group project and the ability to discuss their work. Dispositions to work out problems with others in a group setting, negotiate and express their opinions.

Fountains

Materials:

paper and pencils
resource books about fountains
plastic tubing and sections of hose
variety of funnels
buckets
large plastic dishpans
measuring cups

Preparations:

This project is best done outside
with enough materials for each
group to work successfully or
inside in an area of the classroom
where a water source is available
and one group may work at a time.

Before You Begin:

If possible, take the children to visit a local fountain. Contact the city department
that is responsible for the maintenance of the fountain and see if they could provide
a knowledgeable resource person who would be able to answer questions the children have about how the fountain works. If that is not possible, consider making a
short video showing a local fountain and use it to begin a discussion. Some questions that will be interesting for children to consider include:

How does the water make the spray?
Where does the water come from?
After the water comes out of the spray, where does it go?

Do not feel compelled to answer the questions for the children but rather show
interest in helping them figure out their solutions.

Fountains

Implementation:

Begin by asking each group to work together to design a fountain of their own. Provide the materials and ample time for them to explore the possibilities. Older children may be able to draw their plans on paper before they begin. Your interactions with the group as they work through the process will help them in answering some of the questions that they may have and working through problems and conflicts that may arise. If you are working outside, provide each group with buckets of water to pour through tubing with a large measuring cup or plastic pitcher. Once completed, allow the group to demonstrate their fountain for the others and encourage the classmates to ask questions. Leave the finished fountains available for the children to explore throughout the theme.

Assessment:

Knowledge about how fountains work with water flow, skills in using materials. Language and communication skills in developing ideas, discussing them with others and expressing their point of view. Feelings about working and sharing ideas in a cooperative project. Dispositions to work cooperatively, to work out problems in a group setting, to persist with a project and to be inquisitive about how things work.

What You Need to Make a Fountain

A Base

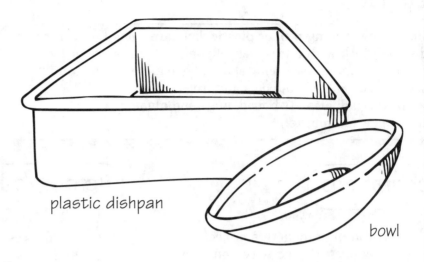

plastic dishpan

bowl

A Water Source

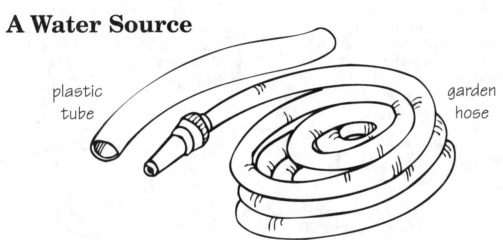

plastic
tube

garden
hose

A Pump

spray bottle

baster

Tadpole Habitat

Materials:

child-size swimming pool or plastic dishpans: one for each group
tadpoles (check with a local school supplier, bait store or a
    nature center where they should be available year round)
resource books about tadpoles and frogs
food for the tadpoles: fish food, bugs and algae
chart paper and markers

Preparations:

If you plan to do this project as a whole group activity, you will use the child-size swimming pool or it may be done in small groups and you will need a plastic dishpan for each group. This activity may be done outside; tadpoles can survive in weather above freezing temperatures.

Before You Begin:

Read a resource book about tadpoles and frogs. Lead a short discussion about your findings afterwards. Include in the discussion the habitats that frogs live in and what frogs would need to survive. Make a list of the responses on a chart.

Implementation:

Begin the project by taking the children outside to gather materials for their tadpole habitats. Discuss how each item may be used. For example: rocks for sitting, sticks for climbing, dirt to make the water like a pond. Allow the children to discuss how to create the habitat and work together to create them. Once the tadpoles are established in their new environment, encourage the children to make observations. Allow the children to set up a schedule for feedings on a chart and post it near the habitat. Add drawing paper and colored pencils to the area, and encourage children to make drawings of the tadpoles as they see each new stage of the tadpole's development. Display the drawings near the habitat for reference.

Assessment:

Knowledge about tadpoles, frogs and their development and needs. Language skills in contributing to group discussions, questioning and expressing an opinion. Small motor development in drawing and large motor development in working outside in gathering materials. Dispositions to care for animals and the environment, participating in a group project and working out problems.

Pontoon Boats

Materials:

Legos®
sand and water table or dishpan
set of small plastic people

Preparations:

Add a basic set of Legos® to the sand and water table.

Before You Begin:

Lead a short discussion about different types of boats. Encourage the children to add to the discussion with types of boats they have seen or been on. Read a book about boats. Introduce a pontoon boat to the children. Discuss some of the features of a pontoon boat.

Implementation:

Assign one small group at a time to work in the water area and use the Legos® to make a pontoon boat. Interact with the children as they work on their design. Ask open-ended questions about how they designed the boat as they test it at the sand and water table. Add small plastic people to the project and encourage the children to see how many people can float on their boat without causing it to sink. Allow the children to bring their designs to a follow-up class discussion to share with the other children.

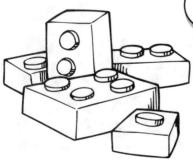

Assessment:

Knowledge about types of boats, floating and sinking and boat design. Small motor skills in using building materials. Language and communication skills in labeling and contributing to a discussion. Dispositions to work cooperatively, persist with a task, solve a problem and negotiate with other children toward a solution.

Where Does Water Come From?

Materials:

large roll of art paper
markers
resource books

Preparations:

Gather the materials in an area of the classroom that will allow a small group of children to work together on a large chart with markers.

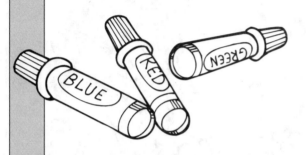

Before You Begin:

Lead a short discussion with the children to start them thinking about how water gets into our homes. Be careful not to impose any opinions of your own, but rather ask the question and allow the children to discuss their ideas.

Implementation:

After the discussion, ask one small group at a time to work together. Have the groups make a diagram on art paper to show where they think water comes from and how it ends up in our homes. Encourage the children to express their opinions to other members of the group. Allow the group ample time to work on the chart. Once completed, allow the group to share their chart and discuss their ideas. Display each group's chart in the classroom for reference throughout the theme.

Assessment:

Knowledge about water sources and how they work. Language and communication skills in expressing ideas to other group members and putting those ideas in visual form. Small motor skills in using art materials. Feelings about a group project and the dispositions to persist with a task and negotiate.

Resources for the Theme of Water

At the Frog Pond, Tilde Michels, Lippincott, 1987

Dark & Full of Secrets, Carol Carrick, Clarion Books, 1984

Environmental Experiments with Water, Thomas Rybolt, Enslow Publishing Co., 1993

Experiments with Water, Ray Broekel, Children's Press, 1988

Experimenting with Water, Bryan Murphy, Lerner Publications, 1991

The Fish: The Story of the Stickleback, Margaret Lane, Dial Press, 1981

A Fish Hatches, Joanna Cole & Jerome Walker, William Morrow Co., 1978

Fish Is Fish, Leo Lionni, Alfred A. Knopf, 1970

Floating & Sinking, Kay Davies and Wendy Oldfield, Steck-Vaughn, 1992

Floating and Sinking, Jerry Jennings, Gloucester Press, 1988

Follow the Water from Brook to Ocean, Arthur Dorros, Harper & Row, 1991

A Frog's Body, Jerome Wexler, William Morrow, 1980

Frog & Toad Series, Arnold Lobel, Harper & Row

The Frog, Angela Royston, Warwick Press, 1989

If You Were a Fish, S.J. Calder, Daniel Weiss Assoc., 1989

Loon Lake, Ron Hirschi, Cobblehill Books, 1991

My Goldfish, Herbert H. Wong and Matthew F. Vessel, Addison-Wesley, 1969

On the Water, Julie Fitzpatrick, Silver Burdett Co., 1985

The Science Book of Water, Neil Ardley, Harcourt Brace, 1991

Simple Science Experiments with Water, Eiji Orii, Gareth Stevens, 1989

Splash & Flow, Ruth Howell, Atheneum, 1973

Swamp Spring, Carol and Donald Carrick, Macmillian, 1969

Water, Water Everywhere, Mark J. Rauzon, Sierra Club for Children, 1994

Waterworks: Water Play Activities, Jeanne C. James, Kaplan Press, 1987

Sorting Collections

Materials:

paper or plastic sacks with handles,
   one for each group
poster board
markers
white glue

Before You Begin:

For this, and most of the projects in this chapter, children will be working in small groups. (See the information about working in small groups in Chapter 3 on page 39.) You will want to form those groups and allow the children to choose a name for their group. Tell the children that they will take a walk with their group to find materials that are outside.

It would be a good idea for you to inspect the area where the children will be walking before they go outside. Remove any dangerous, unsanitary or unsavory materials. You might even want to "plant" a few items for the groups to find. You are the best judge of whether or not this activity is appropriate for your location.

Assessment:

Knowledge about collections and categories, labels of various materials. Language and communication skills in using labels and communicating with group members. Small and large motor skills. Disposition to work cooperatively.

Preparations:

Gather the materials at a table where one small group can work cooperatively.

Implementation:

Give each group a sack for their collections. Take a walk around the school and ask the children to find things that are interesting to put into their sacks. Back in the classroom, provide each group with a sheet of poster board. Ask the children to work together to organize their collections. Allow them to decide how they will categorize the things they found and to manage their own decisions as much as possible. Once the groups have put their collections into categories, provide white glue and ask them to glue their collections to the poster board. They may wish to name their categories, for which you can provide a marker and assistance if necessary. Allow each group to share their poster with the others and display them for future reference throughout the theme.

Language Center Tent

Materials:

small tent or sheet and
   clothesline
books on the outdoors from
   resource page 97
flashlights

Preparations:

Place a small tent in the Language Center or string a clothesline across the center and drape a sheet over it. Use weights or small bags of sand to anchor the four corners. Place the resource books inside the tent along with the flashlights.

Before You Begin:

Read one of the books from the resource list to the class. Invite the children, during center time or a quiet reading time to read the book inside the tent with flashlights. Discuss the number of children the tent will accommodate.

Implementation:

This new experience for reading books should be ongoing throughout the theme. To encourage continued participation, continue to add books after having read them to the class throughout the theme.

Assessment:

Language and communication skills of sharing an oral reading experience, basic knowledge about books, demonstration of stages of reading. Feelings about choosing a book. Dispositions to read books and share them with other children.

Bug Sketches

Materials:

drawing paper
pencils and colored pencils
magnifying glasses
resource books with insects

Before You Begin:

Lead a short discussion about insects common to your geographic area and discuss some of the information the children have about them. You may want to guide children toward looking for specific insects and remind them to avoid others.

Preparations:

Divide the children into pairs and give each pair a clipboard with a sheet of drawing paper and pencils and a magnifying glass.

This project could be done with a few children at a time if you have access to the outdoors from your classroom.

Implementation:

Allow the children to work outside in pairs. Ask each pair to find an insect that they would like to study. Encourage them to work together to use the magnifying glass to carefully study the insect and then to draw it on the paper. Continue to encourage them to work together and to take time to find as many details about the insect as they can. If time allows, they may draw more than one insect. Once back in the classroom, allow the children to use the resource books to see if they can identify their insect from their drawing. Older children may wish to copy information about their insect next to their drawing and label the various parts. Mount the completed work for future reference throughout the theme.

Assessment:

Knowledge about various common insects, labeling of insects, their parts and functions. Language and communication skills in working with a partner, expressing ideas. Dispositions to work cooperatively, make discoveries and take pride in work.

Camping Center

Materials:

small tent or sheet and
  clothesline
sleeping bag
tackle box
paper plates, plastic
  cups, plastic utensils

cooler
flashlights
backpack
boots, fishing vest, hat
first aid kit
picnic basket

Preparations:

At the beginning of this theme, write
a letter to parents explaining the
theme and some of the objectives
for incorporating it into your curriculum. Make a list of the materials that parents might donate.
Gather the materials in the
Dramatic Play Center.

Before You Begin:

Lead a short discussion about camping.
Include the children's ideas about what things are done on camping
trips and what special equipment is needed. Share some of the materials you have
gathered and discuss their purpose.

Implementation:

Have one small group of children work in the Dramatic Play Center at a time.
Have the children arrange the space and role-play a camping experience. Use the
time to observe the children in their interactions with each other as they take on
the various roles they create. This area will continue to develop throughout the
theme. Allow ample time for the children to experience the camp.

Assessment:

Knowledge about camping experiences. Small and large motor skills in using the
materials. Language and communication skills in expressing ideas, working with
others and labeling materials. Dispositions to work cooperatively and take on roles
in dramatic play situations.

Diagram of the School Yard

Materials:

white paper
pencils
large roll of art paper
markers

Preparations:

Gather the materials, one set per group.

Before You Begin:

Take the children for a walk in the school yard and ask them to point out the different areas. Once inside, review the things you saw and discuss them.

Implementation:

Ask one small group to work together at a time to make a diagram, first on the white paper with pencil as a rough draft. Once completed, discuss their draft with the group. Encourage them to share their sketch and make suggestions as necessary. Provide a large sheet of art paper and ask the group to transfer their draft drawing onto the large paper in final form with markers. You may encourage the children to label the various areas, providing assistance as it is needed. Older children may use resource materials to look up the names of objects they are unfamiliar with or shrubs, flowers and trees that are in the area. Once completed, ask the group to share their final drawing with the entire class. Mount each group's work for future reference throughout the theme.

Assessment:

Knowledge about labels of common items. Language and communication skills in labeling, diagraming and discussion with others. Dispositions to work cooperatively, negotiate and problem solve.

Outdoor Still Life

Materials:

variety of materials found in local area
small box
fabric for a drape
copies of page 91
colored pencils

Preparations:

Gather an interesting collection of commonly found natural materials from your local area. For example: pinecones, acorns, interesting leaves, flowers grown locally, fresh fruit or vegetables. Make a display in the center of a table by placing a small box in the center of the table. Drape the box with the fabric and arrange the materials you gathered on the fabric.

Before You Begin:

Share the display with the children and help them identify each item. Share some information about each item that would be interesting to the children.

Assessment:

Knowledge about natural materials found in their area and careful examination of them. Small motor skills of drawing and using art materials. Dispositions to work on an art project and persist with a task to completion.

Implementation:

Allow one small group to work at the project at a time. Give each child a copy of page 91. Ask each child to sit or stand at one side of the table and draw the still life from their perspective in the first square of their paper. As each child finishes, they should move to another side of the table and draw the still life again, only from the new perspective. Continue until each child has drawn the still life from four different perspectives. Share the drawings with the class and mount them on a display for all to enjoy.

Outdoor Still Life Worksheet

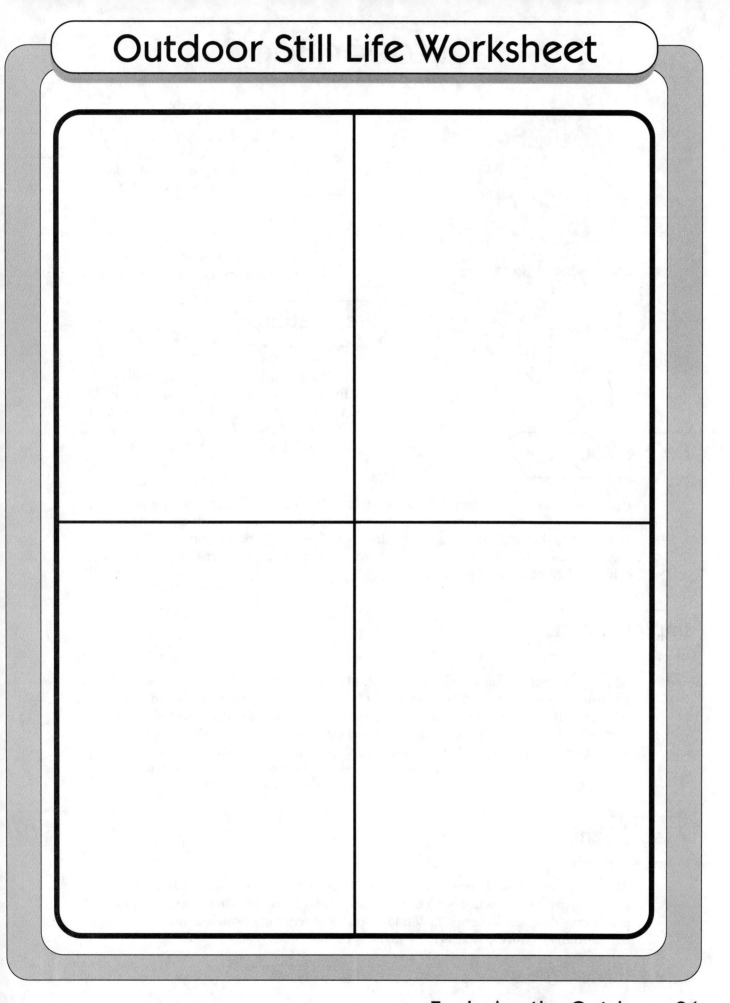

Outdoor Book

Materials:

lined paper or white copy paper
cover stock (poster board, file folders, etc.)
magazines
scissors
white glue
colored pencils or markers

Preparations:

Make a blank book for each group with lined or white copy paper for the inside and cover stock for the outside. Gather the materials at a table where one small group can work together at a time.

Before You Begin:

Read one of the books about outdoor activities from the resource list on page 97 to the children. Lead a short discussion about the book and other things that children know about the outdoors. Introduce the idea of working together in small groups to make a book about the outdoors. Encourage the children to share ideas about the book and possible contents.

Implementation:

Allow one small group to work on a book at a time. They may use magazines for pictures of outdoor activities or draw their own pictures. They can write the book by themselves or with assistance, as necessary. Ask open-ended questions to keep the group thinking about possibilities for their story and title. When each group has a completed book, add their names to the cover as the authors. Allow each group to share their book with the class and display the books for reference throughout the theme.

Assessment:

Knowledge about outdoor activities. Small motor skills for writing and art. Language and communication skills in expressing ideas to others, language in print, knowledge of letters and sounds, stages of writing development. Dispositions to work cooperatively and express themselves.

Trash Patrol

Materials:

copies of the Trash Patrol
   badges on page 95
heavy stock paper
lamination film or clear
   self-adhesive paper
hole punch

yarn
trash bags
disposable plastic gloves
scale
graph paper

Preparations:

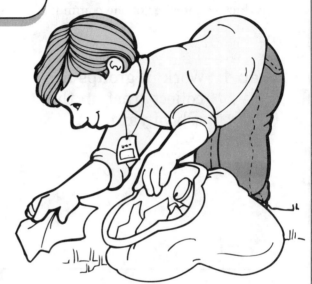

Copy page 95 on heavy stock paper, cut out badges and laminate them or cover with clear self-adhesive paper. Punch a hole in the top of each. String yarn through the hole–the yarn should be long enough to go over a child's head comfortably.

Before You Begin:

Lead a short discussion about litter. Encourage the children to share what they know about litter and the problems it causes for the community. Share the idea of the Trash Patrol, where children will work one day a week in small groups during recess to pick up trash in the school yard. Show the children the Trash Patrol badges and tell them that they will wear their badges during their turn at Trash Patrol.

You may wish to examine the area in advance and remove any dangerous, unsanitary or unsavory items.

Implementation:

Give each Trash Patrol a large trash bag and gloves. Monitor their efforts as they find and pick up trash throughout the school yard. You might check with a teacher of older children to see if they could volunteer to help monitor the children as they work. Return to the classroom and ask the Trash Patrol to discuss their efforts. Ask the children to estimate how much the trash bags weigh. Record the estimations on a chart pad or chalkboard. Weigh the bags and compare the estimations. Start a graph of the amount of trash each Trash Patrol collects and, as they are recorded, make weekly comparisons to the previous recordings on the graph. If possible, make weekly contributions to a local recycling effort. A graph of the amount of the trash that is able to be recycled could be recorded.

Trash Patrol

Knowledge about graphs and recording numbers, counting, making estimations and weight. Large motor skills in working outdoors. Language and communication skills in discussion issues, recording information and communicating with others. Feelings about helping others. Dispositions to work cooperatively and be a productive member of the community.

Step 1: Work in groups to collect trash in the school yard.

Step 2: Estimate and weigh the trash.

Step 3: Graph and compare the results.

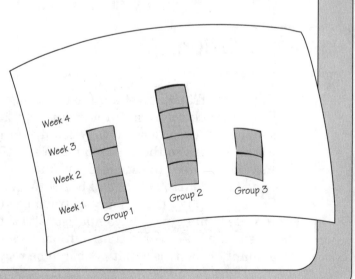

Trash Patrol Badges

Outdoor Cooking

Materials:

grill, charcoal (starter fluid)
food for menus planned
paper and pencils
paper plates, plastic utensils, plastic cups
cooler, ice, juice

Preparations:

You will need adult volunteers for this project. Write a letter to parents, grandparents or contact the education department of a local college or university. It is possible that the home economics department of the local high school may be able to assist with the project.

Before You Begin:

Place each small group at a table with an adult volunteer, paper and pencil. Assign each group a part of a meal to plan. For example: main dish, salad, vegetable, fruit, dessert. Be sure to stress that the items they choose to prepare should be nutritious, serve the entire class and volunteers and be able to be prepared outdoors.

Implementation:

Ask each group to work together to plan their part of the outdoor meal that they will prepare. Write the plans on the paper with the assistance of the adult volunteer. Share the plans in a class meeting and set the date for the meal. Check with your school's food service for help purchasing the food and ask for volunteers to assist. If possible, allow the children to be involved in purchasing the food. On the day of the outdoor meal, allow each group to work with their adult volunteer to prepare their part of the meal. When everything is ready, serve the meal on the paper or plastic products and eat together outside. Choose a book about picnics to read to the group when the meal is complete (see resources on page 97). Clean up the area before returning to the classroom.

Assessment:

Knowledge about food groups, healthy foods, measurement and food preparations. Small and large motor skills in food preparations. Language and communication skills in expressing ideas, recording their ideas and sequencing. Feelings about a shared meal experience. Dispositions to work cooperatively, take on task and communicate effectively to a group.

Resources for the Theme
Exploring the Outdoors

About Garbage and Stuff, Ann Zane Shanks, Viking Press, 1973

Amazing Anthony Ant, Lorna and Graham Philpot, Random House, 1994

Anno's Journey, Mitsumasa Anno, Philomel, 1977

Big Al, Andrew Clements, Scholastic, 1988

Counting Wildflowers, Bruce McMillan, Mulberry, 1986

Curious George Goes Camping, Margaret Rey, Houghton Mifflin, 1990

Deep Down Underground, Olivier Dunrea, Aladdin, 1993

Earth Verses & Water Rhymes, J. Patrick Lewis, Atheneum, 1991

A Garden Alphabet, Isabel Wilner, Puffin Books, 1991

Hiking, Donna Bailey, Steck-Vaughn, 1991

The Icky Bug Alphabet Book, Jerry Pallotta, Charlesbridge, 1986

Insects, Illa Podendorf, Children's Press, 1954

An Insect's Body, Joanna Cole, William Morrow & Co., 1984

Insects & Crawly Creatures, Angela Royston, Macmillan, 1992

A Look at the Environment, Margaret S. Pursell, Lerner, 1976

Miss Penny & Mr. Grubbs, Lisa Campbell Ernst, Aladdin, 1991

My First Nature Book: A Life Size Guide to Discovering the World Around You, Angela Wilkes, Alfred A. Knopf, 1990

Nightmare in My Backyard, Donald M. Silver, W.H. Freeman, 1994

The Reason for a Flower, Ruth Heller, Grosset & Dunlap, 1983

Recycling, Joan Kalbacken and Emilie E. Lepthien, Children's Press, 1991

The Snail's Spell, Joanne Ryder, Puffin Books, 1982

Teddy Bear's Picnic Cookbook, Abigail Darling, Puffin Books, 1991

Trees, Illa Podendorf, Children's Press, 1954

Worm's Eye View, Kipchak Johnson, Millbrook Press, 1991

TLC10046 Copyright © Teaching & Learning Company, Carthage, IL 62321

Nursery Rhymes at the Listening Center

Preparations:

Copy the nursery rhymes on pages 109-114 onto a transparency and enlarge onto poster board. Use markers to color the pictures. Laminate the posters. Make copies of each nursery rhyme, one for each child. Make a tape recording of each of the nursery rhymes read onto blank cassette tapes. Consider having different people read each nursery rhyme for a variety of interpretations. Each tape may include several versions of the same nursery rhyme repeated several times in a variety of voices. For example: the principle, a parent and an older child could be on the same tape reading "Jack and Jill." Gather the other materials listed for the listening center.

Before You Begin:

Introduce one nursery rhyme at a time by having the children repeat it as you point out the words on the poster board. Invite the children to visit the Listening Center to listen to tapes.

Nursery Rhymes at the Listening Center

Implementation:

This open-ended project should continue throughout the theme. Add a new nursery rhyme as the children seem ready for one. Encourage the children to follow along with the words on the poster or their own copy of the nursery rhyme as they listen to the tape. Older children may use the writing paper to make their own copies of the rhyme and add their own drawings. Add children's voices to each cassette tape reciting the rhyme.

Assessment:

Language and communication skills of listening to oral language, listening to pattern in language, following printed words, identifying printed words and sounds, forming letters and words in print. Small motor skills in writing. Disposition to be a reader.

Hickory's Clock

Materials:

collection of a variety of sizes of empty cardboard boxes
tape, glue
tempera paint, brushes, drop cloth or newspapers
variety of art materials
copy of the poem "Hickory, Dickory, Dock" on page 109
poster board and markers
lamination film or clear self-adhesive paper

Preparations:

Enlarge a copy of "Hickory, Dickory, Dock" on page 109 onto poster board, color the pictures and laminate. Mount the poster in the area where the children will be working on the project. This project may work well in the Art Center where the materials are readily available.

Before You Begin:

Introduce the nursery rhyme "Hickory, Dickory, Dock" and ask the children to say it aloud as you point out the words on the poster. Lead a short discussion about types of watches and clocks. Make a list or show pictures of the different types of clocks.

Implementation:

Allow one small group to work on the project at a time. Ask them to use the boxes to make a grandfather clock. Allow the children to work together to decide how to use the materials to make a clock. Encourage them to solve problems by interacting with others. When the clock is complete, allow the group to share it with the class. Each group's clock may be displayed in the room along side a copy of the poem.

Assessment:

Knowledge about clocks and labels of parts and functions. Language and communication skills in printed and oral language, communicating effectively. Small motor skills in using materials. Dispositions to work cooperatively, negotiate and solve problems.

Cooking Miss Muffet's Curds and Whey

Materials:

cottage cheese and mixed fruit (fresh or
   canned)
bowls, spoons
measuring cups and spoons
copy of recipe on page 103 printed on
   poster board
copy of nursery rhyme on page 111
poster board and markers
lamination film or clear self-adhesive paper

Preparations:

Copy the recipe for curds and whey
onto poster board. Gather the materials for cooking at a table where
one small group may work at a time.
Enlarge the copy of the poem on
page 111 onto poster board and color
with markers. Laminate the poster
and mount next to the recipe.

Before You Begin:

Introduce the nursery rhyme "Little Miss
Muffet" and ask the children to say it aloud as
you point out the words on the poster. Lead a
short discussion about the poem and ask the
children what they think curds and whey
might be. (Curds are similar to cottage cheese,
and whey is a liquid by-product of processing
cheese.) Introduce the recipe, shown in individual portions for Curds and Whey.

Little Miss Muffet
Little Miss Muffet sat on a tuffet
Eating her Curds and Whey
Along came a spider
and sat down beside her
frightened Miss Muffet Away.

Implementation:

Work with one small group at a
time. Use the recipe printed on
the poster throughout the
process. Encourage the children
to help follow the recipe by
reviewing each step before mov-
ing to the next one. Once the
recipe is prepared, allow the
group to eat and discuss the
taste. Review the poem "Little
Miss Muffet" again, as they eat.

Assessment:

Knowledge of cooking procedures,
labels, measuring. Language and communication skills in labeling, oral and
printed language, sequencing of concepts and communication with others.
Feelings about food and food preparations. Dispositions to work cooperatively and persist with a task.

Cooking Miss Muffet's Curds and Whey

Miss Muffet's Curds and Whey

1. Wash your hands.

2. Measure ¼ cup (60 ml) cottage cheese into a bowl.

3. Measure 3 tablespoons (45 ml) of fruit into a bowl.

4. Stir with a spoon.

5. Eat your curds and whey.

Jack and Jill at the Sand and Water Table

Materials:

sand and water table or a large plastic tub with sand
copy of nursery rhyme on page 112
lamination film or clear self-adhesive paper
poster board and markers
make a well with: butter tub, sticks, tape
make pails: with caps from plastic bottles
small plastic people

Preparations:

Enlarge a copy of the nursery rhyme "Jack and Jill" on page 112 onto poster board and color with markers. Laminate the poster and mount over the sand and water table. Make a miniature well. Add the bottle caps from plastic bottles (for example: fabric softener bottles) for pails and small plastic people.

Before You Begin:

Introduce the area to the children and ask them to recite the poem aloud as you point out the words on the poster.

Implementation:

Encourage the children to use the materials at the sand and water table for play in reciting the poem "Jack and Jill." Children may make a hill from the sand and use the small plastic people for the parts of Jack and Jill. Interact with the children and point out the words to the poem on the poster as they recite it during play.

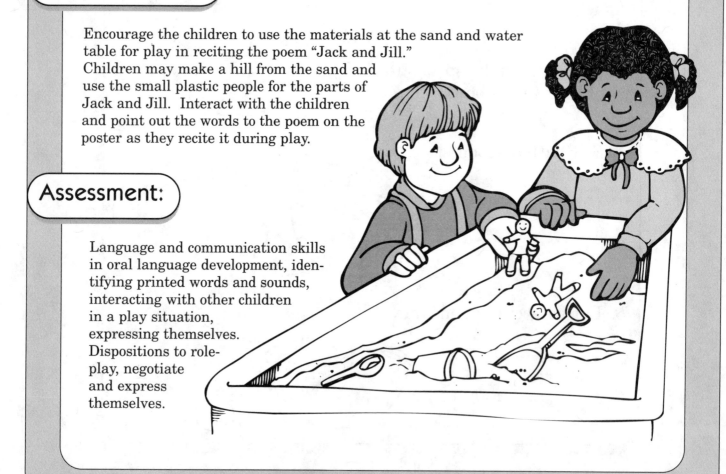

Assessment:

Language and communication skills in oral language development, identifying printed words and sounds, interacting with other children in a play situation, expressing themselves. Dispositions to role-play, negotiate and express themselves.

Mary Had a Little Lamb in the Dramatic Play Center

Materials:

To re-create a school room: desk, chalkboard, paper and pencils, books, map, globe
stuffed animals
copy of the poem "Mary Had a Little Lamb" on page 113
poster board and markers
lamination film or clear self-adhesive paper

Preparations:

Enlarge a copy of the poem "Mary Had a Little Lamb" on page 113 onto poster board and color with markers. Laminate the poster and mount in the Dramatic Play Center. Gather the materials to re-create a school room.

Before You Begin:

Read the poem "Mary Had a Little Lamb" with the children as you point out the words on the poster. Ask the children to imagine what would happen if the little lamb followed Mary to school. Encourage a discussion about a lamb in school. Introduce the area to the children.

Implementation:

Allow one small group to use the Dramatic Play Center at a time. Encourage the children to use the materials for their interpretation of the stuffed animals in school. This area should be ongoing throughout the theme for development of the play.

Assessment:

Knowledge of school policies and procedures. Language and communication skills in communicating with others, printed and oral language, expressing themselves. Feelings about school. Dispositions to work cooperatively, interact effectively, negotiate and role-play.

Humpty's Wall

Materials:

unit blocks
plastic eggs
plastic horses and soldiers
copy of poem "Humpty Dumpty" on page 114
poster board and markers
lamination film or clear self-adhesive paper

Preparations:

Enlarge a copy of the poem "Humpty Dumpty" on page 114 onto poster board and color with markers. Laminate the poster to hang in the Block Center. Gather the materials in the Block Center or create an area where children have ample space to build with blocks.

Before You Begin:

Introduce the nursery rhyme "Humpty Dumpty" and ask the children to repeat it aloud as you point out the words. Lead a small discussion about the information children may have about the wall, the soldiers and why Humpty Dumpty couldn't be put back together again.

Implementation:

Invite the children to work in small groups in the Block Center to act out the poem "Humpty Dumpty" with the unit blocks and other materials. Interact with the children and point out the words of the poem on the poster as they recite it during play.

Assessment:

Knowledge about references in the poem and various labels. Small and large motor skills in using blocks and other materials. Language and communication skills in oral language development, identifying printed words and sounds, interacting with other children in a play situation, expressing themselves. Dispositions to role-play, negotiate and express themselves.

Nursery Rhyme Murals

Materials:

large roll of art paper
markers, colored pencils, crayons
variety of art materials
white glue
magazines

Preparations:

Cut five strips of art paper into large sections. Print on one side of copy of each of the nursery rhymes on pages 109-114. Gather the materials in an area where a group may work together on a mural using art materials.

Before You Begin:

Divide the children into small groups and review the nursery rhymes with the class. Ask each group to choose one of the poems to make a mural.

Implementation:

Allow one group to work at a time. Review the poem with them and ask them to work together to make illustrations for the poem.
Children may choose to draw pictures onto the mural or draw, color, cut out and glue figures or cut out pictures from magazines. Encourage the children to work together to make decisions about their mural and how to depict it visually. As each group completes their mural, allow them to share it with the class and leave it on display throughout the theme.

Assessment:

Knowledge about visuals for interpretation of the poem. Language and communication of oral and printed language, labels, expressing themselves through visuals. Small motor skills in using materials. Dispositions to express themselves, negotiate with others and to work cooperatively in a group. Feelings of pride for a finished product.

Sequencing Nursery Rhymes

Materials:

copies of the poems on pages 109-114
sentence strips
markers

Preparations:

Copy the poems with a visual for each line onto sentence strips.

Before You Begin:

Choose one of the poems to use as an example. Begin by reviewing the nursery rhyme from the poster you have made from a previous project. Point to the words as the children repeat it aloud. Show the class the sentence strips and how each line of the poem is on one sentence strip. Allow the children to assist you in putting the poem in order where all of the children can see it.

Implementation:

Allow one small group to work with one (or more if they seem ready) set of sentence strips for a poem. Encourage the children to work together to get the lines of the poem in order, saying it aloud as they work. Add more poems as the children show interest. Work with them if they struggle to associate the words of the poem with the printed version. Use the sentence strips on a sentence strip chart when working with the class.

Assessment:

Knowledge of words in print, sound associations, sequencing of a familiar text, oral language. Dispositions to work cooperatively, express feeling and become a competent reader.

Hickory, Dickory, Dock

Hickory, dickory, dock;
The mouse ran up the clock;

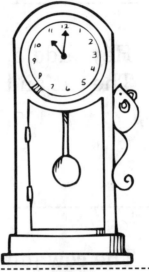

The clock struck one,

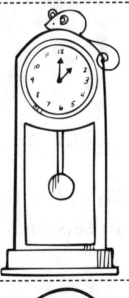

The mouse ran down,
Hickory, dickory, dock.

Hey, Diddle, Diddle

Hey, diddle, diddle,
The cat and the fiddle,

The cow jumped over the moon;

The little dog laughed
To see such sport,

And the dish ran away
   with the spoon.

Little Miss Muffet

Little Miss Muffet sat on
her tuffet,

Eating her curds and whey.

Along came a spider
And sat down besider her,

And frightened Miss Muffet away.

Jack and Jill

Jack and Jill went up the hill,

To fetch a pail of water;

Jack fell down and broke his crown,

And Jill came tumbling after.

Mary Had a Little Lamb

Mary had a little lamb

With fleece as white as snow,

And everywhere that Mary went

The lamb was sure to go.

Humpty Dumpty

Humpty Dumpty sat on a wall.

Humpty Dumpty had a
great fall.

All the King's horses
And all the King's men

Couldn't put Humpty Dumpty
together again.

Here lies Humpty Dumpty He was a good egg.

Resources for the Theme
Nursery Rhymes

The Alaska Mother Goose, Shelley Gill, Paws IV, 1987

Black Mother Goose Book, Elizabeth Murphy Oliver, Dare Books, 1981

Chinese Mother Goose Rhymes, Robert Wyndham, Philomel Books, 1968

The Comic Adventures of Old Mother Hubbard & Her Dog, Tomie de Paola, Harcourt Brace & Co., 1981

Four & Twenty Dinosaurs, Bernard Most, HarperCollins, 1990

The Glorious Mother Goose, Cooper Edens, Macmillan, 1988

London Bridge Is Falling Down, Peter Spier, Doubleday, 1967

Mother Goose, Fred Crump, Jr., Winston-Derek Publishing, 1990

Mother Goose, Tomie de Paola, G.P. Putnam's Sons, 1985

Mother Goose: A Collection of Classic Nursery Rhymes, Michael Hague, Henry Holt & Co., 1984

Mother Goose's Little Misfortunes, Leonard S. Marcus and Amy Schwartz, Bradbury Press, 1990

Mother Goose Magic, Kay Chorao, Dutton Children's Books, 1994

Mother Goose, Words of Wit & Wisdom, Tedd Arnold, Dial Books 1990

Old Mother Hubbard and Her Wonderful Dog, James Marshall, Sunburst Book, 1991

The Random House Book of Poetry for Children, Jack Prelutsky, Knopf, 1983

Random House Book of Mother Goose, Arnold Lobel, Random House, 1986

Read Aloud Rhymes for the Very Young, Jack Prelutsky, Knopf Publishing, 1986

Scared Silly! A Collection of Stories, Rhymes, Riddles to Laugh Your Fears Away, Marc Brown, Little Brown & Co., 1994

Side by Side: Poems to Read Together, Lee Bennett Hopkins, Simon & Schuster, 1988

Talking Like the Rain, X.J. Kennedy and Dorothy M. Kennedy, Little Brown & Co., 1992

Where the Sidewalk Ends, Shel Silverstein, Harper & Row, 1974

Chapter 9

An Amish Farm

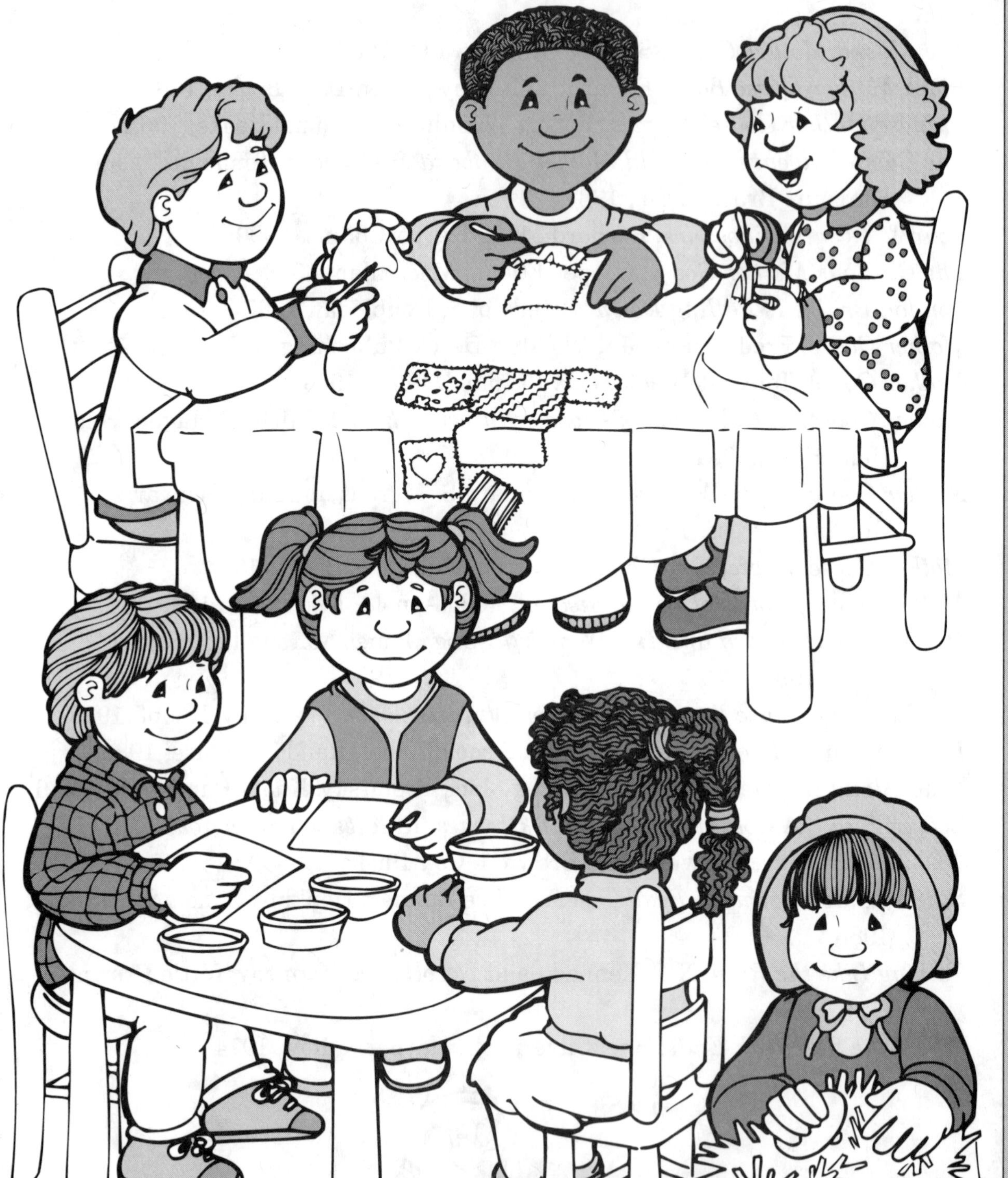

Cooperative Barn Building

Materials:

empty cardboard boxes
tempera paint, brushes, drop
  cloth or newspapers
variety of art materials
scissors

Preparations:

Gather the materials
in the Art Center of
another area where
one small group
can work togeth-
er using art
materials.

Before You Begin:

Divide the children into small cooperative
groups that will work together throughout
the theme. Allow each group to give themselves a name. Make a chart of the group
members and the name they chose to be
posted where you hold class meetings.
(See more information about working in
groups in Chapter 3 on page 39.) Lead a
short discussion about barns, including
their purpose and function. Explain that
the Amish often build a barn for their
neighbors by working together. Discuss
the benefits of this way of working.

Assessment:

Knowledge about barns, farms, animals
and their functions. Small and large motor
skills in using the materials. Language
and communication skills in expressing
ideas, communicating with others, labels
and descriptions. Dispositions to work
cooperatively, role-play and negotiate.

Implementation:

Ask one small group to work in the
Art Center (or another area where
you have gathered necessary supplies) to build a barn. They may
use a box as a base. Use a craft
knife to assist in cutting out open-
ings for doors and windows as
necessary. Encourage the children
to work together to make decisions
about how their barns are con-
structed. As each group finishes
their barn, allow them to share it
with the class and discuss their
work. Allow the group to use the
barns in dramatic play. Add small
plastic or wooden animals, people,
tractors and fence. Or, as a follow-
up, allow the groups to make these
things from art materials.

Quilt Making

Materials:

white sheet
large-eye plastic or metal needles in a pin
    cushion
yarn or embroidery thread
scraps of fabrics
scissors

Preparations:

Gather the materials at a
table where a small group
of children can work.

Before You Begin:

If possible, locate a local quilt-maker who would be willing to come to the school to
share some of her quilts and discuss her art with the children. Or bring a quilt to
demonstrate and spark interest. Encourage the children to examine the quilt and
discuss the variety of fabrics and shapes that were used.

Implementation:

Allow one small group to work on the quilt at a time, rotating until every child has
had at least one opportunity to participate in the quilt making. Spread the white
sheet on a table. Assist the children in choosing fabric patterns, cutting them out
and using the large-eye needles to sew them onto the sheet. Continue until the
sheet is covered with fabric. Keep a chart to show the number of days the quilt
took to complete. Display the quilt in the classroom or on a hallway display along
with a sign showing the number of days it took to complete.

Assessment:

Knowledge about quilts and how they are made. Small motor skills in threading a
needle, eye-hand coordination. Language and communication skills in discussing the
project with others. Feelings of pride in contributing to a group task. Disposition
to persist with a cooperative project.

Seed Collage

Materials:

variety of seeds, including: corn,
    wheat, oats, barley
cardboard squares cut to a uniform
    size, one per child
white glue
yarn
scissors
butter tubs with lids (one for each type
    of seeds)

Preparations:

Place the different types of seeds in
butter tubs with lids. Prepare a space
where a small group of children can work at
a table together, sharing the materials. Cut
lengths of yarn approximately 6" to 8" (15 to 20 cm)
long. Make an example of a seed collage using a cardboard square as a base, yarn glued to form sections and
seeds glued within each section.

Before You Begin:

Lead a short discussion about collages. Show an example of other
types of collages and the one you
made from seeds. Help the children
identify the types of seeds used.
Discuss how to use the yarn to create
sections for the seeds.

Implementation:

Allow one small group of children to
work at a time to make a collage from
the variety of seeds. Encourage the
children to label the types of seeds they
are using. Set aside the finished collages to dry overnight. Once they are
completed, display the seed collages
together with labels for the variety of
seeds used.

Assessment:

Knowledge about different types of seeds. Small motor skills in using small tools.
Language and communication skills labeling and interactions with others. Feelings
about art projects. Disposition to persist with a task to completion.

Baking Pies

Materials:

ingredients for making cornstarch clay
    (see recipe)
rolling pins
wooden cutting boards
variety of pie pans, glass,
    aluminum—small and large
play dough

Preparations:

Make the cornstarch clay ahead of time and store in an air-tight container. Gather the other materials in a Cooking Center or large table where a small group can work together.

Cornstarch Clay

1 cup (240 ml) cornstarch
2 cups (480 ml) baking soda
1¼ cups (300 ml) water

Mix and cook over med-lo heat until thick. Cool and knead. Air dry. Store in an air-tight container.

Before You Begin:

Lead a short discussion about pie making. Make a list of the variety of pies that the children have eaten. Introduce the project of working with clay (not edible) to make pretend pies.

Implementation:

Encourage the children to explore the possibilities when working with the clay. Allow them to roll the clay with rolling pins on the cutting boards. Encourage pretend pie making, using the clay for pie dough and the play dough for fillings. This project may be ongoing throughout the theme for children to return to for additional explorations.

Assessment:

Knowledge and labels for different pies, food groups, nutritional information. Small motor skills in using the rolling pins. Language and communication skills in labeling and discussion with others. Feelings of pride. Dispositions to persist with a task, role and pretend play.

Popping Corn

popcorn (Indian corn) and other varieties of corn
large pan with lid and hot plate or popcorn popper
oil, butter, salt
large bowl, wooden spoons
small paper bags
copy of *The Popcorn Book* (see resources on page 128)
chart paper and markers

Preparations:

Check with a local grocery store or farmers' market to find ears of popcorn. If possible, buy other types of corn to demonstrate the variety of corn that is grown. Gather the materials in an area where children can work with food.

Before You Begin:

Read *The Popcorn Book* aloud to the children and lead a short discussion about popcorn. Allow the children to discuss information about how popcorn is produced. Introduce the ears of corn. Allow the children to hold and compare the different types of corn. Discuss their uses and by-products.

Implementation:

Work with one small group at a time. Review the information from the book about how the kernels pop. Ask the group to help decide on a recipe to follow for making their own popcorn. Record the recipe on chart paper and mount it in the center, referring to it as you proceed. Begin by allowing the children to remove the corn from the ears. (Skip this step if you are using purchased popcorn.) Follow the recipe dictated from the children. Refer to the print on the chart and review each step as you proceed to the next one. When the popcorn is ready, allow the children to distribute sacks to other groups and their own. While they enjoy the popcorn, encourage the children to review new information they learned about popcorn.

Assessment:

Knowledge about popcorn, other types of corn, corn products, cooking procedure. Language and communication skills in sequencing, following written and oral directions, reviewing information, communicating with group members. Dispositions about participating in a group activity, expressing ideas and sharing information.

Farming Book

Materials:

white typing paper
cover stock (poster board, file folders, etc.)
staple
crayons, colored pencils
magazines
scissors
white glue

Preparations:

Make blank books by stapling several sheets of white paper with a sheet of cover stock on the outside. Gather the materials at a table where children can work together.

Before You Begin:

Lead a short discussion about information you have learned about farms. Read one or more of the books listed on the resources page (page 128) that provide information about farms.

Implementation:

Allow one small group to work together at a time to make books about farms. Provide each child with a blank book. Encourage the children to locate, cut out and glue pictures into their book that show scenes typical of farms: including animals, equipment, people and foods. They may also draw pictures to include in their book. Encourage children to attempt to write captions for pictures. Provide assistance if necessary. When the books are complete, allow each child to read their book to the others. Place the books in a Language or Book Center for others to enjoy throughout the theme.

Assessment:

Knowledge about farms and terms and labels associated with farms. Small motor skills in using materials, including cutting skills. Language and communication skills of communicating ideas in printed form, stages of writing development and oral languages skills. Disposition to communicate through written form.

Woodworking Center

Materials:

woodworking table
wood scraps
tools: hammer, saw, vice
sandpaper, nails or tacks
safety goggles

Preparations:

A Woodworking Center works best on a commercially produced table designed for this type of work. Materials made available on a pegboard, where they are easily accessible to children, will make the area run more smoothly. Store wood scraps in a box or plastic tub under the table.

Before You Begin:

Introduce the Woodworking Center to the children leading a short discussion about the names of the tools and their purpose. Encourage the children to discuss possibilities of projects they could make with wood and how important a woodworking area is to farmers. Discuss a safety issue with the children. Set a limit on the number of children that will be available to work in the area at a time and stress wearing goggles.

Woodworking Center

This area will provide the greatest benefit to the children if it is available for exploration throughout the theme. In the beginning, your goal for the children should be an opportunity to explore how the tools work with wood. As the children become more familiar with the materials, they will begin to think of projects they can make and complete. You may encourage them to add buildings, fences and animals to the barns that were made in Cooperative Barn Building on page 117. Add wood glue, paint and brushes as the projects dictate. As projects are completed, share them with the other children and encourage them to be used in other areas or displayed.

Assessment:

Knowledge about functions of tools. Small motor skills in coordination, eye-hand motor control. Language and communication skills in labeling materials, expressing ideas and discussing sequence of work. Feeling of pride for finished projects. Dispositions to organize a project, persist to finish a project, problem solve and find solutions.

*You can learn more about the set up and management of a Woodworking Center in *Center Time: A Complete Guide to Learning Centers*, Dana McMillan, © 1994, Teaching & Learning Company, Carthage, IL 62321.

An Amish Breakfast

Materials:

ingredients for each recipe (see page 126)
utensils necessary for each group recipe
paper plates, utensils, cups
chart paper and markers
copies of the recipes on pages 126

Preparations:

For this project you will need to have the children divided into four groups with an adult to assist with each group. Contact your parents, grandparents or the high school's home economics class for volunteers. Provide a space for each group to work. Print each recipe onto chart paper and gather the ingredients and utensils necessary for each group. Review the recipes with the adult volunteers and discuss how to help the children.

Before You Begin:

Lead a brief discussion about meals that would be typical for families that live on a farm. Check the resources on page 128 for resources about foods produced on farms. Encourage the children to share what they know about foods that are locally grown.

Implementation:

Ask each adult volunteer to review their recipe with the children, discussing each step. Encourage them to allow the children to participate as much as possible. For example, measuring ingredients, stirring, pouring. When the food is prepared, allow the children to set the table and sit together to eat their breakfast along with the adult volunteers. Lead informal discussions with the children as they eat, sharing what they learned during the food preparations.

Assessment:

Knowledge about food, nutrition and measurements. Small motor skills in using cooking utensils. Language and communication skills in following directions both oral and printed, communicating with group members and expressing ideas.

Amish Farm Breakfast Recipes

Copy this page and distribute to each group.

Amish Cornbread

2 cups (480 ml) cornmeal
1 teaspoon (5 ml) salt
1½ teaspoons (7.5 ml) baking soda
1½ teaspoons (7.5 ml) baking powder
1 tablespoon (15 ml) sugar
2 eggs
1½ cups (360 ml) buttermilk
¼ cup (60 ml) cooking oil

Heat oven to 400°F (204°C). Sift dry ingredients together. Stir in eggs, buttermilk and cooking oil. Pour into greased 9" x 9" (23 x 23 cm) pan or muffin tins. Bake 30 minutes.

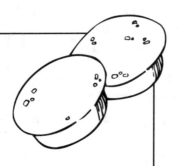

Amish Cornbread Syrup

1 cup (240 ml) light corn syrup
½ cup (120 ml) brown sugar
½ cup (120 ml) water
½ teaspoon (2.5 ml) maple flavoring
½ teaspoon (2.5 ml) vanilla
1 tablespoon (15 ml) butter

Cook and stir syrup, sugar and water until the sugar dissolves. Stir in flavorings and butter. Serve warm.

Butter

Add a clean marble to a baby food jar filled half way with whipping cream. Place the lid on securely. Allow each child to shake the jar until butter is formed. Pour off excess liquid by washing the butter in cold water and draining. Repeat process of washing the butter several times. Add salt if desired.

Fresh Fruit Cups

Variety of fresh or locally grown fruits: peaches, pears, oranges, bananas, apricots and strawberries. Wash and peel fruit. Cut into bite-sized pieces. Mix in large bowl with wooden spoon. Place in small bowls and serve.

Gathering Eggs

Materials:

plastic eggs
straw or Easter egg grass
baskets with handles
shoe boxes
dress up clothes for the farm, including:
 hats, bonnets, overalls, aprons

Preparations:

Gather the materials in the
Dramatic Play Center. Place the
shoe boxes on a low shelf or table.
Fill each shoe box with straw or
Easter grass. Place several plastic eggs in each shoe box. Arrange
the clothes where children can
get to them.

Before You Begin:

Lead a short discussion with the children about hens, chickens and eggs. Read a
book from the list of resources on page 128. Show the children the materials gathered in the Dramatic Play Center and discuss their purpose.

Implementation:

Allow one small group to work in the Dramatic Play
Center at a time. Encourage the children to dress in
the clothes and do chores associated with farming,
like gathering eggs. Allow the children to role-play
the various jobs of the workers on the farm as
they understand them, and use the opportunity
to further their understandings in informal
conversations. Allow this project to change
and add new materials for additional activities throughout the theme.

Assessment:

Knowledge about roles of farm workers, labels and understanding of materials
associated with a farm. Language and communication skills, interacting with
group members, expressing ideas and communicating effectively. Dispositions to
role-play, work cooperatively, negotiate and problem solve.

Resources for the Theme
An Amish Farm

Across the Stream, Mirra Ginsburg, Mulberry, 1982

Amos and Susie: An Amish Story, Merle Goode, Good Books, 1993

Anno's Counting Book, Mitsumasa Anno, HarperCollins, 1975

Apples and Pumpkins, Anne Rockwell, Aladdin, 1994

Corn Is Maize: The Gift of the Indians, Aliki, HarperCollins, 1976

Country Fair, Gail Gibbons, Little Brown & Co., 1994

Down Buttermilk Lane, John Sandford, Lothrop Lee & Shepard, 1993

Egg Story, Anca Hariton, Dutton Children's Books, 1992

Farmer Duck, Martin Waddell, Candlewick Press, 1991

Farming, Dennis B. Fradin, Children's Press, 1983

A Farmyard Song, Christopher Manson, North-South Books, 1992

The Folks in the Valley: A Pennsylvania Dutch ABC, Jim Aylesworth,
        HarperCollins, 1992

Friends, Helme Heine, Aladdin, 1986

How Do Apples Grow? Betsy Maestro, HarperTrophy, 1992

I Can Be an Animal Doctor, Kathryn Wentzel Lumley, Children's Press, 1985

Just Plain Fancy, Particia Polacco, Bantam, 1990

Mr. Grumpy's Outing, John Burningham, Holt & Co., 1970

Mouse's Birthday, Jane Yolen, Putnam's & Son, 1993

My Farm, Alison Lester, Houghton Mifflin, 1994

The Popcorn Book, Tomie de Paola, Holiday House, 1978

The Pumpkin Patch, Elizabeth King, Dutton Children's Books, 1990

Pumpkin Pumpkin, Jeanne Titherington, Mulberry, 1986

Prairie Alphabet, Jo Bannatyne-Cugnet, Tundra Books, 1992

Reuben and the Fire, Merle Goode, Good Books, 1993

Seasons on the Farm, Jane Miller, Prentice-Hall, 1986

Zinnia & Dot, Lisa C. Ernst, Viking
        Children's Books, 1992

Chapter 10
Communicating with Parents

Communicating a Developmental Assessment Program

Chapter 1 of this book introduced a discussion of developmentally appropriate practices and the implications for designing an assessment program for young children. This chapter will continue to explore those issues as they relate to how educators communicate with parents/care givers.

The key to effectively communicating a developmental assessment program is that information is always centered on the child; comparing him *only* to himself.

There are four types of opportunities to communicate with parents:

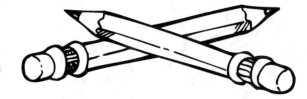

Formal Written Communication:

Monthly newsletters; letters of introduction to the class and the school; letters to communicate goals, curriculum, upcoming events, monthly calendar of events.

Informal Communication:

Discussions before and after school, at social times in and away from the school.

Formal Communication:

Presentations at an open house; parent/teacher meetings; curriculum nights; presentations for school board, administrators, at educational workshops.

Scheduled Parent/Teacher Conferences:

Held two or more times during the school year for the express purpose of discussing a child's progress.

It is critical that clear communication during all of these opportunities is consistently focused on the development of the individual child, avoid comparisons to other children in *any way*.

Kindergarten Parents' Monthly

October

Focus: Center for October

This month we will focus on **The Art Center**. We began this center in September with very basic supplies: construction paper, colored pencils and crayons; adding new materials as the children's projects demanded. Most recently we have added a box filled with a colorful array of yarn. Suddenly, the projects (as I'm sure you've noticed) have included lots of glued yarn pieces.

One popular task in **The Art Center** is always easel painting. During our 45-minute center time, you will always see two children busy creating a picture with tempera paints. These paintings are beautiful, but they also show me the children's interests and their ability to depict these interests in pictures. There is often a story told along with them. When you see my writing at the bottom of the picture, you will know that those words were dictated by your child, telling me what we should know about the painting. As children develop more understanding about words and sounds, they may begin to write their own descriptions which make this painting experience a language development activity as well.

Theme Update: The Body

We are continuing our theme of **The Body** this month. The children are learning so much about their bodies and healthy practices. The hospital we have set up in the Dramatic Play Center is very popular. The children love to weigh themselves and measure their height for the *treatment sheet* that is filled out for entry to the hospital. They have learned about height in inches (centimeters) and feet (meters) and are developing some clear ideas about weight. If you have any materials that could be added to the hospital that you would be willing to donate, they would be appreciated. We especially need more ace bandages (we always have a lot of sprained ankles and wrists!) and clean, empty pill bottles.

Parent/Teacher Conferences

You will be receiving a form to fill out for a time that is convenient for you to attend a Parent/Teacher Conference in November. I will look forward to having an opportunity to talk to you about your child's development and have you share information that is important for me to know.

September _____

Dear Parents,

I am pleased to introduce myself to you and welcome your family to our school. My name is Mary Susan Blockley, and I will be your child's teacher.

My love of children and working with families and the joy of seeing young children develop in every area is why I chose to become a teacher. This will be my 12th year as an early childhood educator. Every year at this time, I think about how much I look forward to a new beginning and getting to know the families of the children I will work with in my class.

I believe that every child wants to learn and develops new skills and information in an individual way. My job is to encourage those interests in learning in your child and to share as much information as possible with you about our progress. But this is not a "one way street." It is very important that you are able to share with me all of the important information you have about your child. Our talks together will be just that, sharing information between us and I look forward to those times.

Each month you will receive a newsletter to keep you informed about things we are learning, areas of interest and ways you can help at home. If you have any questions or concerns, please let me know immediately, so we can discuss them and come to a decision that is best for your child. Throughout the year you will be invited to attend a parent information workshop to learn more about our curriculum and to ask any questions you may have about what your child is learning. I hope you can attend as many as possible.

I am looking forward to meeting you personally.

Sincerely,

TLC10046 Copyright © Teaching & Learning Company, Carthage, IL 62321

Formal Written Communication: Curriculum Update

Dear Parents,

Next month we will begin a theme on The Post Office. I have chosen this theme because the types of projects I've designed will encourage the development of writing. It is important for you to know that at this stage in your child's development, spelling and hand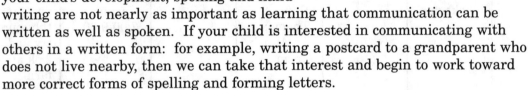writing are not nearly as important as learning that communication can be written as well as spoken. If your child is interested in communicating with others in a written form: for example, writing a postcard to a grandparent who does not live nearby, then we can take that interest and begin to work toward more correct forms of spelling and forming letters.

Learning about the post office will also offer an opportunity to learn about communities and jobs, addresses, sorting and how the mail is delivered. To begin the theme, a large box will be delivered to our classroom. It is a surprise and children will have a fun time trying to guess what is in the box and who sent it. We will take a trip to the local post office where the children will be able to see, firsthand, how the mail finds its way to our homes.

You can help me with this theme in several ways:

- If you have business at the post office, take your child along and point out some of the areas and how they work.

- Collect old junk mail, cancelled stamps and postcards and send them to school with your child. We will be setting up our own post office, and we need a lot of mail!

- I would love to have a special visitor come to the classroom who collects stamps and would be willing to share his/her collection with the children. Do you know of someone with this interest who would relate well to young children? If so, please call or send me a note.

Our post office theme is sure to be an exciting learning opportunity for all of us. I will continue to keep you informed.

Sincerely,

Pre-Kindergarten Calendar for February

Sunday	Monday	Tuesday	Wednesday	Thursday	Friday	Saturday
1	2 Library books due	3 Music	4 Cooking Day Theme: An Amish Farm	5 Gym	6 School Carnival 7:00-9:00	7 Take a drive in the country and look at farm animals
8	9 Library books due	10 Music	11 Field trip forms due	12 Gym	13 Field trip to the farm	14 Go to the library and look for books on farms
15	16 Library books due	17 Music	18 Parent/ Teacher meeting: 7:00-9:00	19 Gym	20 Early dismissal: Teachers' workshop	21 Check out a children's video with a farm theme
22	23 Library books due	24 Music Eat Lunch with Your Child Day	25 Grandparents' Day: Make butter	26 Gym	27 Field trip to farm section of zoo	28 Make popcorn

Informal Communications

Informal communications are times when you and the parent have a conversation which is not scheduled. These opportunities are not formal, not long in length and need to focus on positive information about current activities. Avoid trying to solve major problems in this setting.

During an informal communication you can:

- Discuss the child's day: How did he do after the parent left? Is she feeling better after having been at home with an illness? Did she take a nap, eat a snack or lunch or seem tired in the afternoon? Some schools develop a Daily Communication Form for this type of information. But even if it is written, parents will often wish to have a quick update from the teacher.

- Relate a new development for the child: The child had his first experience in helping set the table for snacks and proved to be a great helper. He walked on the balance beam in the gym for the first time unassisted and was so pleased with himself he even drew a picture to show his new accomplishment.

- Help the child discuss an issue with the parent: A child was unable to reach the toilet in time and was very upset and embarrassed. You talk with the mother and the child helping her tell the part of the story she seems to want her mother to know and demonstrate a supportive, caring demeanor.

- Encourage a parent with whom you have been working: Share with the parent that her efforts to read with her child are making a difference. Relate that her child is showing a real interest in reading books at the Language Center on a regular basis.

Maria

Mike

Apple

Keesha

Formal Presentations

Workshops for parents are an excellent way to communicate to parents about how their children learn and develop, the school's curriculum goals and how parents can assist with their child's learning in appropriate ways.

Some possible topics for these formal presentations:

- Stages of Development: Based on Piaget's stages of development with specific information about the pre-operational (ages 2 to 7 years) child's characteristics, interests and skills.

- Stages of Language Development: Specific information about how a child develops reading and writing through predictable stages that teachers can demonstrate and parents can identify.

- Mathematical/Logical Thinking in the Young Child: Information in practical ways about how a child begins to understand math concepts in visual and concrete ways before beginning to use formal math problems.

- What a Child's Play Shows Us About His Social Development: Help parents understand the value of play situations for the classroom and dispel the myth that play is not learning and why.

- Teaching Using Themes: The value of choosing themes based on a child's interest and how well-chosen projects allow teachers to integrate learning into meaningful activities for the child.

Special Tips for Parent Workshops:

Survey your parents for the best night and time to present the workshops.

Make an agenda (see page 137) and keep to it, even if you have to leave something out.

Make the workshop active. Adults, too, like to learn in an interactive way and don't want to spend their evenings in long lectures.

Provide a snack or ask the parent/teacher organization to help out with cookies or muffins.

Formal Presentation: Example of an Agenda

Topic: Mathematical/Logical Thinking

7:00-7:10   Welcome and introduction of the topic by principal

7:10-7:25   Overview of the topic with overhead projector and transparencies showing examples of the key points by teacher

7:25-7:30   Divide the parents into groups and assign them to a task set up around the room by another teacher

Three Tasks for helping parents see a practical way in which math and logical thinking are used by young children:

Estimating Volume
Sand and water table filled with sand, beans or rice; variety of containers; funnels; and paper and pencils. Ask parents to determine which containers hold an equal amount, more or less and record their information to share with the group.

Survey and Graphs
Clipboard with blank paper, pencils, graph paper and Unifix™ cubes. Ask parents to survey the group and record the eye colors of everyone in the group. Make a chart on graph paper using the Unifix™ cubes to share their findings.

Measurement
String, scissors, poster board and markers. Ask parents to make measurements among their group members to find out if the height of a person is the same as their arm span, more or less. Work together to show the findings on poster board.

8:00-8:30   Ask each group to share their discoveries, discuss their task and draw conclusions about how the task benefits learning

8:30-8:50   Questions and answers with teachers and administrators available to answer specific questions by parents

8:50-9:00   Dismiss, talk informally

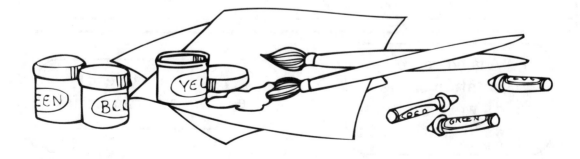

Parent/Teacher Conferences

A diagram of an effective parent/teacher conference:

Parents and teacher seated on the same side of the table

Away from other distractions like phones and clocks

A good representation of the child's work that best shows his/her growth

A table (not desk) free from other materials

Do's and Dont's for Parent/Teacher Conferences

Do's:

Schedule times with the parents and write them a note to confirm the time and then stick to the schedule. If you anticipate a conference that will need additional time, make that adjustment in your schedule.

Place adult-size chairs in the hallway to make a comfortable waiting area. Add some materials that parents may find informational to look at while they wait. For example: children's work, back issues of parent newsletters or tape recordings of the children reading their favorite books.

Keep the information centered on the child and any accomplishments since you last spoke.

Ask the parents to contribute their thoughts and observations about their child, particularly as they relate to the child's feelings about school and his own learning.

Make notes about any concerns you have and be direct but positive.

End the conference on time and on a positive note.

Don'ts:

Send out a notice and expect that if parents want to talk to you, they will call.

Meet in a small meeting room off the principal's office.

Use this opportunity to tell the parents that their child is "so far ahead of the other children"

Talk for 24½ minutes, look at your watch and say, "We only have about 30 seconds left; did you have anything you wanted to ask me?"
Wait until the parents are in the hallway and then say, "Oh, by the way, there is one other problem."

Get so far behind that you have half of the families waiting in the hallway.

Resources

Achievement Testing in the Early Grades: The Games Grown-Ups Play, Constance Kamii, National Association for the Education of Young Children, 1989

Beyond Self-Esteem: Developing a Genuine Sense of Human Value, Nancy E. Curry and Carly N. Johnson, National Association for the Education of Young Children, 1990

Developmental Screening in Early Childhood: A Guide, Samuel J. Meisels, National Association for the Education of Young Children, 1987

Emerging Literacy: Young Children Learn to Read and Write, Dorothy S. Strickland and Lesley Mandel Morrow, International Reading Association, 1989

Engaging Children's Minds: The Project Approach, Lillian G. Katz and Sylvia C. Chard, Ablex Publishing Corporation, 1989

First Grade Takes a Test, Miriam Cohen, Dell Publishing, 1980

The Hurried Child, David Elkind, Addison-Wesley Publishing, 1981

Listen to the Children, Docia Zavitkovsky and Katherine Read Baker, National Association for the Education of Young Children, 1986

Reaching Potentials: Appropriate Curriculum and Assessment for Young Children, Volume 1, Sue Bredekamp and Teresa Rosegrant, National Association for the Education of Young Children, 1992

A Practical Guide to Alternative Assessment, Joan L. Herman, Pamela R. Aschbacher and Lynn Winters, Association for Supervision and Curriculum Development, 1992